PRAISE FOR
MAKERS IN A THINKERS' WORLD

Please receive my dear friend Amy's grounded and intense challenge to find the creative freedom your soul, and every soul, is thirsty for... she is a trustworthy guide on this topic. Let your full self come alive to God in new ways through her invitation!

—***Mindy Caliguire,*** *president, Soul Care*

* * *

Makers In A Thinkers' World is a magnificent work of art. Each page pulls you in and takes your breath away. You can almost feel the gentleness of a breeze on your face while reading Amy's beautiful words. Here is a fresh perspective on creativity, spiritual life, and spiritual transformation that will engage, inspire, and energize you in such a way that you will look at spiritual life with a renewed lens. This book is not simply a sit-down-and-read project. Here you have a practical, reflective, peace-infused experience that refreshes and blesses you. Amy's honesty and transparency are invigorating. Her stories are compelling. You will be glad you took the time to enjoy this book.

— ***Chris M. Coursey,***
THRIVEtoday President, Author of *The Joy Switch*

* * *

In *Makers in the Thinkers' World*, Amy Pierson skillfully guides us as we reenvision the definition of creativity. And here is her delightful message: creativity is not for a chosen few. All of us are lovingly created and given the gift of expressing that creativity for our good and the benefit of others. Through interactive experiences, brain science, and solid spiritual formation, Amy invites us to discover and cherish our hidden maker within. Engage your whole self in connection with God as you enjoy this book!

— *Gem Fadling*
Founder of Unhurried Living, Inc.
and author of *Hold That Thought*

* * *

I love the thought that my creativity is part of the unique gift package I bring to the table to help fulfill the Great Commission! Amy Pierson's book, *Makers in a Thinkers' World,* will make your soul dance and dazzle your mind with the possibilities of creative expression in every area of life. Amy's focus on the neuroscience behind creativity is a welcome breath of fresh air that can break the self-isolating creative boxes we construct. You will especially enjoy the Maker Exercises at each chapter's end. They will help you engage with God—the first and ultimate Creator. I can't recommend *Makers in a Thinkers' World* highly enough.

— *Ed Khouri*
President, Equipping Hearts for the Harvest
and author of *Becoming a Face of Grace: Navigating Lasting Relationship with God and Others* and *The Weight of Leadership: How Codependency and Misplaced Mercy Undermine Your Life and Leadership*

* * *

Makers in a Thinkers' World is a brilliant handbook packed with old and new treasures. Amy Pierson pulls from her rich family history and deep dives into spiritual formation and her joy-filled discovery of paradigm-shaking insights into interpersonal neurobiology, neurotheology, and attachment theory. She has brilliantly released a pathway of convergence between the thinkers and the makers, the logical and the creative. Amy authentically shares the story of her childlike cry for a more experiential and embodied life with Immanuel, the God who is with us and creates with us. She has become like a proverbial Mary Poppins who has flown in on the winds of change currently shaking the Western church and family. And because of heritage and her childlike heart, Amy has spread a magnificent feast merging the children's table with the grown-up table with burning prophetic insight and heartfelt honor for her family's spiritual legacy. Within each chapter, she pulls from her carpet bag another magic insight and activation, empowering us all into an authentic, relational, and creative transformation. If your heart is burning for this freedom and integration, I challenge you to gather some of your family and her table and go fly a kite with Amy and her friends. I certainly plan to.

— ***Kent Larson,***
founder and director of RadiusNetwork.org

* * *

Makers in a Thinkers World is a unique and valuable guidebook to help understand and draw out your inherent creativity! Amy's lyrical insights and the treasure trove of inspiring exercises she's curated will help makers everywhere "discover and express more of our true and creative selves.

—***J. Scott McElroy,*** Author, *Creative Church Handbook, Finding Divine Inspiration,* and Director, New Renaissance Arts.

* * *

Amy Pierson has done what very few people can - she's woven together a beautiful tapestry of spirituality, science, and practical advice that inspires the reader to become a "maker." Even if you already consider yourself an artist of some kind, this book will reinvigorate and enlighten your process. Amy's writing is a gift, and I am so glad it exists in a world where deep creative activity is sorely needed.

— ***Quinton Peeples,***
writer, director, and producer

* * *

Have you ever thought of yourself as more of a right- or left-brained person? This book takes you through a series of adventures with the Word of God and both sides of your brain, constituting a whole-brain experience. Amy paints word pictures in such an engaging reading experience you won't be able to put this down. These and other of her teachings cause spiritual reverberations throughout the body of Christ as people like me continue to learn from her to open our eyes and ears of conference audiences. Learning to fully engage with both the right and left hemispheres is a powerful step toward the integration of living a whole-brain life. This book helps us begin to hear and see it, that is, if we haven't already.

—***Annabelle Wallneau,***
vice-president of Lance Wallneau Ministries

MAKERS
IN A
THINKERS' WORLD

MAKERS IN A THINKERS' WORLD

What Brain Science Teaches about the Spiritually Transforming Power of Creativity

AMY HOWEY PIERSON

Foreword by Dr. Jim Wilder

MAKERS IN A THINKERS' WORLD

Published by
Illumify Media Global
www.IllumifyMedia.com
"Let's bring your book to life!"

Paperback ISBN: 978-1-959099-43-7

Typeset by Art Innovations (http://artinnovations.in/)
Cover design by Debbie Lewis

Printed in the United States of America

Dedication

For Bill, Whitney, Haley, Tanner, Judah, and Thea
Of all God's blessings, you are my greatest delight

"I will give thanks to the LORD with my whole heart;
I will recount all of your wonderful deeds."

PSALM 9:1 (ESV)

CONTENTS

FOREWORD

I am borrowing an image from the prophet Isaiah to describe Amy, the artist growing up in the company of amazing Christian intellectuals who focused on spiritual formation. These great minds around her searched diligently for lasting truths about life with God. The creative Amy discovered true life with God in ways that were not commonly practiced. She grew up like a tender shoot out of dry ground—a maker in a world of thinkers.

Amy longed to make, create, express, know and be known as a deep part of her faith. Catholic and Orthodox circles have long explored God's mysteries through the arts as a focus for contemplation and meditation. Protestant churches in the West did not seem to consider creativity like Amy's to be a serious contributor to spiritual formation.

Today, I see new generations of Christians rising who—like Amy—appreciate what thought leaders have contributed to spiritual formation yet share the sense that something is missing. They seek a connection with God that feels like a live and authentic exchange that can create in them who they are made to be.

For those longing for spiritual transformation, what are we up against?

When the brain gets information in the form of nerve impulses, it looks first for old recognizable patterns not new, creative thoughts and experiences. During the day, brain circuits are consolidated, establishing patterns (neuropathways) in our white matter. For instance, I do not think about where the keys are on the keyboard (though I once did) because the pattern for typing is well-established, insulated with myelin, and restricted to as few nerves as possible. This specialization process keeps us from creativity or variety because it does the same thing each time. Under stress, *new* images and patterns are the first things the brain lets go of. Old is comfortable. This fact alone can leave artists, inventors, original thinkers, and creatives feeling blocked, vulnerable, and undervalued. Even internally, creatives encounter creative resistance.

Now the good news:

When nighttime comes, the brain dreams. This is its creative time. During dreams, the brain tries all kinds of new combinations and options. Dreaming is the brain working to *avoid* becoming a creature of patterns and prediction—one that cannot think, see, understand, and discover anything new. People who remain curious about the world and the minds of others build upon this creative freedom during their waking hours. Amy calls these adventuring minds "makers."

The brain is intent on its need to create. The reality is few things have been made that could not be improved. God's first comment about creation was that it was good. But upon reflection, God said, "It is not good for man to be alone," and creativity began once again.

Could it be that if we over-develop linear thinking patterns and fear that what we create will not be good, we become like dry ground instead of tender shoots? Amy leads us into and through the common blockages to creativity onward to a more robust life of creative engagement with God, ourselves, and others—thinkers and makers alike.

Let me close with this thought.

I've known Amy for going on ten years and have had the delightful experience of attending and teaching many of her workshops on creativity and Christian spiritual formation. As a clinical psychologist and neurotheologian, I enjoy that she backs up her empowering message with practical brain science.

In Sparking Joy—one of the printmaking workshops I was part of—we were asked to carve a design into a rubber eraser. I can't tell you how fun and freeing that exercise turned out to be—and it felt more profound than the nostalgic thought: *Oh yeah, I remember enjoying this kind of thing as a kid.* In fact, when I was working on my taxes a few months later, I randomly picked up that eraser, and it made me smile.

What appeals to my creative side, however, is music. A few weeks after reading Amy's book, I bought a multi-track digital recorder, put a Tolkien poem to music, and recorded myself playing instruments on different tracks. The creative interaction with his words deepened my experience. And it was fun!

If you are like me, Amy's message will change you. How will it change you? That remains to be seen. Whether you elevate intellectual pursuits over creative connection, don't know how to integrate creativity into your life with God, or are a frustrated creative who feels like your calling isn't taken seriously within the church, this book offers much freedom. Wherever you fall on the left-brain or right-brain dominance——*Makers in a Thinker's World* will inspire new growth into the person you are meant to become.

—E. James Wilder, Ph.D
Chief Neurotheologian at Life Model Works
Author or coauthor of seventeen books including
Living from the Heart Jesus Gave You, *Escaping Enemy Mode*, *Renovated*, and *The Other Half of Church*

ACKNOWLEDGMENTS

I sit on our patio. It is late May, and an uncharacteristically snowy early spring has given way to a verdant green Colorado landscape. The birds seem exceptionally enchanting this morning, as if they know what I'm writing and want to help. Indeed, their joyous trills underscore my gratitude for all those who are in some way part of this book.

As I think about each person and their role in my journey (whether they realize their part or not!), a swell of warmth washes over me. Many have let me postulate and experiment, dream and enact, play and inform in the process of exploring the integrated identity of a maker in a thinker's world. They have shared the best of their creative selves in helping me discern my own. In doing so, we share community.

Jim Wilder, God's graciousness in making us friends—and your graciousness in spending hours answering my questions—leaves me astounded. The life you and Kitty so generously invited me into fueled an ongoing creative renovation of faith in me. It is no understatement to say that your genius, wisdom, dry humor, and generosity have grown my relationship with Jesus and made this book possible.

Ed Khouri, you were once a friend of a friend, and now I am thrilled to have you as one of my own. Thank you for deepening my concept of community and clarifying the gift of grace through our work together. You live what you lead.

Bob Howey, Sr., your entrepreneurial, ageless heart to "get the Church out of a ditch" inspired my own questions: "Why is connection between believers so difficult?"; the direction of my vision: "What if things could be different?"; and my own quest: "How do we get it done?" Your wisdom and encouragement have guided the flourishing and formation of so many—me included. Thanks to you and Mom for investing in my life with God. I love you, Dad.

I am so grateful to Burning Heart Workshops artists, champions, and others who saw the maker spark of God in this book and gathered around to support and encourage. These prayerful visionaries and makers in their own right include: Laura Greiner, Sue Alexander, Sandy MacPherson, Mindy Caliguire, April Diaz, Kent Larson, Theressa McMorris, John and Linda Maikowski, Gem Fadling, Jan Johnson, Jenny Freeman, Molly Urso, Kristi Johnson, Carin Huebner, Christa MacFarlane, Gayla Irwin, Ellen Petti, Cari Jenkins, Sue Shehan, Kay Morrison, John Woods, Ryan Adamson, Talia Thomas, Sara Goodyear, Teresa Weesner, Steven Homestead, Nancy Buschart, Jen Mote, Becky Heatley, Scott McElroy, Merritt Onsa, Julie McKnight, Jean Blackmer; the Melissas (Schaap and Pedigrew); Karen Kelly and Debra Komodore (The Wonder Collective of amazing creatives); Susan Anderson, Shari McDuffy, and Lisa Upman (my Sarasota girls). You have believed in and abided this project for years with me. Thank you for your wholehearted and holy contributions to this soul-expanding work. You are a beloved community.

I am also grateful for the countless transformational friendships that have resulted from the ministries of the Spiritual Formation Alliance, The Downing House, Soul Care, Transforming Creatives, Life Model Works, Thrive Today, Dallas Willard Ministries, Renovaré, Transforming Creatives, and Unhurried Living. God's creativity becomes you.

Supercoach Karen Bouchard, who helped me strategically place stepping-stones across the river of my maker mind, you are a masterclass of grace and skill. Thanks for your invaluable help keeping this book moving!

INTRODUCTION

I was sitting with my friend Jan at a retreat center in the Rocky Mountains. The top floor of the stone building had an oversized corner guest room that lent itself to space for spiritual direction—my friend's specialty. Tall wooden windows opened outward on this beautiful summer afternoon to let in the cooler air that signals the end of most August days at that altitude, along with a bird's eye view of the deer herd that grazed three stories below.

I'd been sharing the experiences over my life's course, particularly the aftereffects of a two-year certificate program that dove deeply into Scripture, the history and historical figures of Christianity, philosophies of spiritual formation, and soul care.

These weren't new topics to me. In fact, before entering the program, I'd spent ten years working with pastors and leaders devoted to Christian spiritual transformation. I engaged with many key thought leaders, and time with them was rich and educational. I followed the counsel and leadership of our founder (my dad, incidentally), board members, and champions. I became familiar with major spiritual formation seminaries, ministries, and churches that were pursuing what it means to be disciples of Jesus. In those ten years, I created events, convened conversations, arranged book tours, and hosted roundtables around the country. My years in this role were truly God's training ground for me and the cornerstone to the frame of my spiritual foundation.

Following that season with a two-year study program on spiritual formation was supposed to tie up all that enlightenment with a neat little bow. I felt pretty well-cooked on the topic.

Cooked and a bit dried out.

* * *

I grew up in the church. In Marge Thomlinson's first grade Sunday school class at Westminster Presbyterian, I accepted Jesus. A few years later, I was baptized (several times to keep it fun) by a worship leader named Willie at the Camp Farthest Out pool during a sweltering summer family camp in Nebraska. Over the course of my life, I'd been Bible-studied, youth-grouped, small-grouped, mentored, and spiritually directed for years. I *knew* the Bible, and I *knew* Jesus. Thanks to my parents and their involvement in the Christian community (locally and around the country), I *knew* many people who *knew* a lot about Jesus, too.

But I didn't know or recognize *me;* that is to say, I didn't recognize people in my circles who connected with Jesus the way I did.

As long as I can remember, I have loved Jesus. As a child, I wanted His name to be beautiful to the world. I wrote poems and songs, created Scripture-related illustrations and greeting cards to remind friends of God's love and sense of humor. God and I talked, and He guided most everything I made. And, as I grew, I just kept doing it.

My personal walk with God was very interactive. At the risk of sounding "woo woo," it was more experiential and embodied. From an early age, I tried to capture impressions, look for a different meaning, convey stories He told me. In more off-script, off-cue, off-hymnal spontaneous—and I believe inspired—ways, I looked to connect with

God and people deeply. Because I recognized His promptings and, for a Presbyterian, was wildly comfortable with the Holy Spirit's still small voice, I *anticipated* interaction.

Along the way, I kept an eye out for anyone who looked like me (or saw me) loving Him a little differently. At a certain point—since I didn't find others openly seeking Him in similar ways—I gave up. I figured the way I connected with God was something quirky for the Lord and me to enjoy together. For a long time, it was enough; but down deep, I had a sense that I needed the company of others in this process. I was lonely. Still, my times with Jesus were wonderful. I came to consider these ways like sitting at the children's table. (So where were the other kids?)

Years later, when I began officially working in the area of Christian spiritual formation, I logged plenty of hours "studying," hoping I could spiritually discipline myself enough to be promoted to sit with the adults at the grownup table. Maybe no one else would see the difference, but I'd feel it and know that I'd arrived.

Spoiler alert: I never got promoted. *Pheew!* Eventually I realized the world I aspired to join seemed more to me like brittle roadside brush—and nothing like the beautiful, messy, vibrant garden I craved.

Nonetheless, there I was: full of God's Word, His words to me, and a creative mind to do something with it. . . but no one with whom to talk and work it out.

This book is for "my people," the Jesus followers like me I looked for in vain for so many years, Jesus followers I now know exist and may be feeling as lonely as I did. This book is about how you and I can leverage our creativity—making life with God even more robust.

This book is also for those wonderful, cherished people I envisioned at the "grownup table," people who love the traditional ways of engaging with Jesus and may not know how to engage with those of us who are more right-brain dominant. After reading this book, you may have a new appreciation for what you can create… and who knows? You may even discover a hidden maker part of yourself.

Thinkers and makers, our superpower lies in our attentiveness to God and one another. Ignited by burning hearts, united around a common cause, we are called not just for ourselves but for the overarching story of God in our life and the life of the Church!

Kind of a big deal, I'd say.

Here's to a joyfully integrated life with Jesus!

I cheer you, makers (and willing thinkers).

Now, let's go save the Church.

HOW TO USE THIS BOOK

Overview

Makers in a Thinker's World is structured to honor the lateralization of our brain function. While the whole brain is necessary for healthy, collaborative function, certain processes and functions tend to be dominant within either the right or left hemisphere.

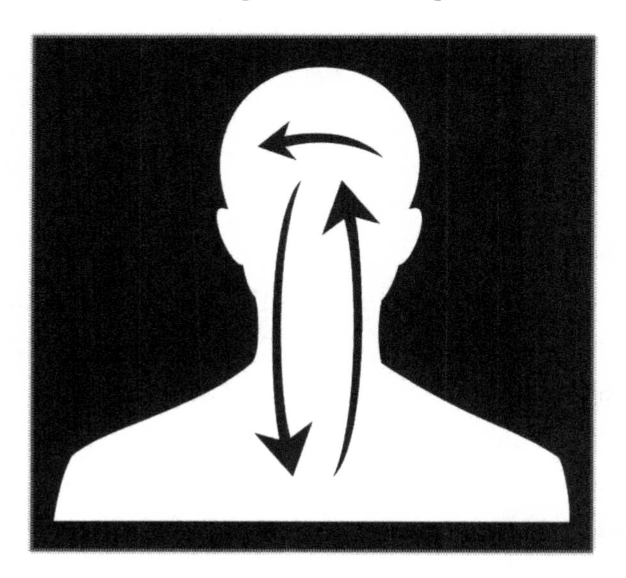

Nerve impulses enter the bottom of the brainstem and move to the top. They fire in a cycle from bottom to top and right hemisphere to left. Interestingly, while circuits on both sides of the brain participate, right-brain functions (emotions, relationships, discernment) are processed quickly at one-sixth of a second, while left-brain functions (knowledge, information, logic) process more slowly at one-fifth of a second. We might say that the right brain knows what is happening before the left.

And this is one of the reasons we are wise to engage our right brain when it comes to experiencing life with God.

In other words, traditional linear means of teaching miss right-hemispheric opportunities to transform character, values, emotions, and relationships.

The following chapters are ordered to engage our right-brain characteristics. Doing so ultimately helps us overcome the relational roadblocks which would otherwise thwart personal creativity, spiritual transformation, relationships, and our part in the Great Commission.

In addition, this book includes a variety of interactive experiences designed to engage your right brain while encouraging meaningful interaction with God.

Here are the interactive experiences you'll find in each chapter:

Visio Divina

You'll be invited to enter a Visio Divina (sacred reflection) using featured art for each chapter. Lectio Divina (sacred reading) is an ancient Christian practice of reading Scripture and allowing God to speak into Scripture. Much the same, Visio Divina uses art and Scripture to draw our attention to God and his character. Engaging all our senses and a robust imagination, we experience new facets of who He is. Pulling from chapter themes and Scripture, you are encouraged to prayerfully turn on the eyes of your heart and imagination as you listen for any insights God may give. Fun fact: all but two of the artists are friends of mine—people whose creative lives inspire mine—proof that there are makers all around us!

For a more vibrant interaction with the art, I encourage you to visit AmyPierson.com. There you will find a full-color version of each artist's work.

Maker Affirmation

Each Maker Affirmation explores an aspect of our soul's creativity. Combined, they provide a new way of considering what it means to be a maker. Repeat these daily to remind yourself who God made you be.

Maker Exercises

Every chapter is followed by a study guide digging deeper into the ideas through personal experience—an opportunity for "Making it Real."

Quieting and Gratitude

Quieting practices help turn off the noise of our left hemisphere and other distractions of life by providing ways to move out of our action-oriented sympathetic nervous system ("fight, flight, freeze, fawn") into the calm of our parasympathetic nervous system ("rest and digest"). Regularly practicing favorites among them can lower stress and fear responses, improve breathing, build resilience, reengage the brain's relational circuits, and relax the body and mind.

Gratitude is a powerful force for joy and peace in our lives. The fullness of life with Jesus depends on the growth of our gratitude capacity. The goal is reconnecting—emotionally, physically, and mentally revisiting—with the people, things, and experiences that bless our life and memory. As we do, you and I acknowledge the Giver. We dig more deeply into the specifics of *why* and *how* in Chapter 8 but invest yourself in these critical exercises throughout the book.

Quieting and gratitude cultivate awareness of our physical, emotional, and spiritual state. In the process, you and I "prime" our mental canvas and ready ourselves for whatever joyful venture lies ahead. I can't encourage you enough to begin every day with quieting and gratitude. Furthermore, returning to these practices throughout the day can help keep us at our maker best, maintaining and repairing things that may otherwise disrupt our peace and purpose.

If you don't remember anything else, practice quieting and gratitude as a regular part of your time with God and His Word. These practices are potent for building communities of joy!

Maker's Prompt

This is your prompt to "make something." Freedom is yours as you use the creative medium of your choice to explore Scripture, metaphor, meaning, and mood sparked by the Maker's Prompt.

Online Resources

You are invited to dig even deeper into the topic of each chapter by visiting my website, AmyPierson.com. There you will find the following:

Left-Brain Warm-ups

Left-Brain Warm-up exercises are available anytime—especially for days when your left brain won't get out of the way or you need a creative kick-start. These are designed to take the self-imposed pressure off you. Just play.

Creative blocks, "impostor syndrome," or the false conviction that we "aren't creative" can get the best of us. After all, these are the "muscles" most likely to be pulled if we don't prepare for a creative workout. Stretching them prepares the rest of our spirit for the remaining creative exercises. Feel free to insert your own warm-ups if you've got them. As one instructor told me, "It is the time we take to get the 'ick' out of our work before we move on to the real work of creating."

Playlists

Nothing lights up the brain like music, so I've created a playlist centered on the themes of each chapter. The first song is always an instrumental selection for your Quieting Exercise. The remaining songs are for your enjoyment as you explore the Maker's Prompt. Feel free to edit and add to what's here or build your own.

Spiritual Disciplines

Here you can find and explore traditional spiritual disciplines with a maker twist. For those unfamiliar, this is an opportunity to experiment with life-giving ways of drawing closer to God modeled by Jesus and throughout Church history. Each provides a great example of integrating more creativity into life with God.

Making More Quieting and Artist Demos

Need more direction about the quieting exercises or still want more creative instruction? Artist demo videos are available to help you experiment with different art media. These are hosted by one of our featured artists or me.

Visio Divina

FOR CHAPTER 1

Banksy, *Rage, the Flower Thrower* (2003),
graffiti mural, Beit Sahour, West Bank, Israel.
(Credit: Atthias Kestel / Alamy Stock Photo)

READ.

Read the following passage aloud to understand its overall meaning.

> I call to you, God; all day I call.
> I wring my hands, I plead for help.
> Are the dead a live audience for your miracles?
> Do ghosts ever join the choirs that praise you?
> Does your love make any difference in a graveyard?
> Is your faithful presence noticed in the corridors of hell?

> Are your marvelous wonders ever seen in the dark,
> your righteous ways noticed in the Land of No Memory?
> I'm standing my ground, God, shouting for help,
> at my prayers every morning, on my knees each daybreak.
>
> **PSALM 88:9–13 (MSG)**

REFLECT.

Read the verses again, highlighting any words or phrases that strike you.

How does this speak to you, today? Listen to this lament without hurry.

REIMAGINE.

When you're ready, turn your attention to *Rage, The Flower Thrower* by Banksy. Consider the passage in the context of this mural.

Along with many cities, Denver has a graffiti festival every summer, as well as year-round guided graffiti tours. In the backstory of many of these murals is a visual lament.

The artist, Banksy, offers us a succinct example in his mural, *Rage, The Flower Thrower*, shown at the beginning of this chapter. The piece confronts the long-standing Israeli-Palestinian conflict. The artist-activist, Banksy, depicts a terrorist in black and white acrylic on a Jerusalem wall. Instead of throwing a Molotov cocktail, hand grenade, or rocks at his enemy, he is throwing a bouquet of flowers—the only color in the mural.

Take your time to consider with God what grieves you:

- What injustice or wrong hurts your heart that you want to "flower bomb"? Allow yourself to be with the feelings that arise for a moment.
- Lament is pain laced with hope. What hope or desire surrounds your lament? Ask the Lord for a vision of what it would look like if God redeemed your lament. How does your creativity lend itself to that vision?
- Who else may share the same lament?
- How can you join God and serve with others to bring change or blessing? What is one practical way you can do?
- What "graffiti" would you like to make?

RESPOND.

Art creates interaction. Prayerfully respond to the Lord about your interaction with His Word and the mural. Journal your responses. Then, contemplate what you've received. Thank God for His faithfulness to meet you here.

CHAPTER 1
CREATIVE ACTION

"When we make, we invite the abundance of God's world into the reality of scarcity all about us."
– MAKO FUJIMARA, *ART & FAITH: A THEOLOGY OF MAKING*

Early on, back in the dawn of COVID-19, most of the US was watching from afar as cruise ships drifted off both coasts, and rumors began rumbling in the media about mass casualties expected in places like Seattle and New York City.

Advised to stay home, there seemed to be a shared ethos of unnerved duty—at least initially.

New to lockdowns, people were suffering with only mild insanity at that point, but projections of extended isolation coupled with soaring infection rates began to cause a deep inner unrest. A palpable fear seemed to roll across our land, complete with the fog of conflicting numbers, conspiring world powers, inaccessible PPE, and—maybe the greatest terror of all—no toilet paper. (I found myself wishing the politicians and newscasters could somehow be forced to gargle hand sanitizer. But I digress.)

Was it the virus, though? Or did we all just have more time to think?

Throw in the murder of George Floyd along with presidential election antics and the Molotov cocktail of social unrest was poured. America was both shaken and stirred.

Sometime during those days, early COVID but pre-murder, I listened to an online panel hosted by the Trinity Forum entitled "Creativity and

Lament." Something panelist Andy Crouch said continues to peal in my heart: "The seed of genuine creative action is lament."

DING! DING! DING! Stop and think about that.

Alongside Jesus, shouldn't that be what we are looking for? Something that energetically/heatedly/actively/catalytically calls our heart to creative action? The purpose that underlies a rewarding life—a vibrant heart for God—must most certainly spring from this germ. Joy and sorrow cross paths at this most purposeful intersection.

And it matters. Profoundly.

But how do we get there? Crouch's words point the way. You and I must plant seeds.

Doing that might require us to first wade into very personal pools of grief. As human beings, we do that by splashing in our own tears, as well as the tears of others. It is where we will begin to discover our creative purpose.

Grief

In 1969, Swiss-American psychologist Elizabeth Kübler-Ross came up with what is now accepted as the five stages of grief. The stages include: denial (disbelief or numbness), anger, bargaining, depression, and acceptance.

Even if we find ourselves overwhelmed at times, we must allow ourselves to sink into the stages of grief. If it is not our grief but another's we observe, it is important to learn how to hold space for their sacred sinking—their ultimate cries of lament give voice to the purpose of their loss. As we allow for and honor their lament, we both come out on the other side a little more whole. The wound is cleansed and the process of redeeming that pain is underway.

My grief came from years of feeling called but unseen. In the introduction to this book, I shared about feeling like I was often being relegated to "the children's table." The unfortunate thing is that I didn't realize *I* had seated myself there until I was in my forties.

From an early age, I wrongly believed that my way of connecting with God—which included journaling, sketching, painting, writing poetry and songs—wasn't "legitimate." Somehow, I picked up the vibe from the people around me that how I engaged with my faith was "cute," but not nearly as important as solid apologetics, theology, study, and service to the poor.

Yet these same people would ask me to use my creative skills to promote ministry events—making invitations, for example—which often left me feeling unseen and used. When creativity is viewed as a means to an end, the point becomes the final product rather than the experience of engaging with God and others in the process. It created a strange wedge between other people and my heart, mind, and true identity.

As someone who thrives on the experience of connecting with God in creative process, I not only felt misunderstood, dismissed, and invisible, I also began to feel dissected from personal passion and cut off from intimate godly relationships.

I carried these feelings about myself and my calling throughout my childhood, into my parenting and especially into my role as a professional. These feelings struck at the heart of what I thought I had to offer God and others. As a result, I kept working harder to get smarter so I could earn a seat at the "grownup" table. In the process, I lost my passionate vision along with my voice. As the word would come to me in prayer years later, if I wanted to get my voice back, I would need to *integrate* what I had orphaned.

Do you hear the loss? Worth grieving, I'd say.

In our own assorted ways, we all suffer loss. By virtue of our gifts, economic status, gender, skin color, or faith community we cut off parts of ourselves that we need to grieve and then reclaim in order to be whole. In *A Grief Observed,* C. S. Lewis aptly wrote, "No one ever told me that grief felt so like fear." Maybe that is why we distance ourselves from it.

Recognizing grief is where we begin.

As much as I wish it weren't true, none of us gets out of this baptism of tears. We left the Garden of Eden long ago, after all. But honestly, is a life without tears really our objective?

Someone once said, "If you love much, you grieve much." For Christians, love is *the* goal. Each step we take to work through our grief(s) gets us closer to a purposeful finish. The steps we take aren't linear—they don't happen in neat, consecutive order.

In addition, what grieves me should never be compared with what grieves you. Grief is not a competition but a call to compassionate attention.

Life gives each of us plenty of material. It is up to us to acknowledge and honor the ache of things lost along the way; to take notice of our own griefs every step of the way to healing. And, by the way, healing doesn't mean we forget the pain. But, when you and I live integrated lives, we no longer fear or avoid grief. Instead, we bring our griefs, wounds, and weaknesses into the light of God's joy (more on that later!).

Several years ago, I took part in a spiritual formation program. Methodist pastor Trevor Hudson was one of my instructors. While protesting apartheid in South Africa with Nobel prizewinner Desmond Tutu and other church leaders, Trevor and the group was arrested and imprisoned. His lament was clarified in the wake of apartheid.

I remember him sharing a story that ended in the wise words of one of his mentors, pastor Gordon Crosby: "Always remember: the person next to you is a pool of tears."

His words ring in my ears with compassion, as do these: "Tears don't have to end in sadness and pain. As different as our pools of tears may be, they can lead us into a new space of change and growth. If we allow our tears to tell their stories, they can become the means by which our lives are transformed."[1]

Despite the noise and hustle of our modern lives, you and I must guard space to become acquainted with our griefs. We must recognize what they are and how they feel in our body, mind, and spirit if we expect to stay the creative course of Jesus' way (Isaiah 53). This vulnerable space cracks open our souls in ways that hold promise to change the world.

Tears not Fears

Culturally, why are you and I afraid of grief? Why does the idea of voicing honest lament seem to embarrass us?

In our very Western way, I think we fear grief because—at the root—we are irrationally afraid of suffering and embarrassed by the emotions it brings up. Vulnerability is unwelcome here. But these fears of exposure are a learned condition. To this day, there are places in the world where lament is instigated when someone dies. In those societies lament is publicly honored and ritualized as a way of life.

Several years ago, my husband and I visited Israel. On the day we were leaving to return home, as we sat outside our hotel near the Western Wall, we heard gunfire and saw helicopters chop-chopping overhead.

With just enough time to catch lunch before our flight, we stopped by the front desk to see if there was any cause for concern.

"You should probably leave for the airport now," a concierge told us, explaining that a famous Orthodox rabbi died and that a citywide processional would slow traffic. Hungry, we decided to take our chances by catching a quick lunch before heading to the airport.

When we hailed a cab to head to the airport, our driver informed us due to abandoned cars on the road, we would have to take a back way to Tel Aviv.

That's when we learned more about the importance of grieving rituals in that country. In accordance with ultra-Orthodox Judaism, a person must be buried on the day of their death before sundown. To honor the dead, Orthodox Jews all over the city stop whatever they are doing and begin walking to the neighborhood of the departed to accompany the body to the cemetery. As a result, the freeways were clogged with empty cars.

At the airport, every TV was tuned to the news. A massive crowd—more than 700,000 people—had turned up in the rabbi's neighborhood. The prayer-laden, clothes-tearing, wailing procession to the burial site took six hours!

Rabbi Ovadia Yosef was reputed to be one of the wisest of his generation, a spiritual leader and statesman who championed Middle Eastern and North African Jews—but (usually on a much smaller scale for most people) this is how grief is observed in their culture. Loss is unabashedly embraced and acknowledged by the community. The sacred sorrow of who and what has been lost is brought out in the open. The result is the impartation of identity and meaning to a well-lived life. A legacy of hope.

Grief Observed

Trust me, I am not endorsing the idea of wallowing in pain. The idea is to allow the hope of God to redeem that pain. To the extent that you and I are willing to notice our life's grief, we can authentically and creatively move toward the God-given hope it reveals. God is looking for those who will pay attention. He is speaking all the time through His Word, our circumstances, His still small voice, creation, even others that He puts in our path. But in order to hear Him, we must *turn aside* from all that distracts us in order to *really* listen. Do you and I expect Him along the way? It is for our benefit, yes, but it is for the benefit of the world He loves so very much. You and I will find power and creative purpose as we respond to our unique ache.

In his book, *Beauty Will Save the World,* Brian Zahnd writes:

> "Sorrow is a necessary consequence of loving others and being fully engaged with humanity. If our plan is to go through life minimizing pain and avoiding as much sorrow as possible, we will do so as a shallow people, and Jesus has nothing to announce to us in the second beatitude—he simply leaves us in our prosaic self-contentment. It is through the work of grief that we carve depth into our souls and create space to be filled with comfort from another."

Avoiding pain, grief, and lament does us no favors. Numbness and contentment are not just shallow, they are life-stunting—spiritually, emotionally, physically, and relationally.

So, here we begin. Very intentionally, we start by quieting ourselves to connect ourselves—body, mind, and spirit—to God. Taking a mental pause for holy noticing, we anticipate hope.

If we do not know how to season our grief with Spirit-led hope, an honest, mourning mentor can help. We may need help digging through the rubble of our religion and stifled emotions to find words. We will discover our words in a strange land somewhere between a birth and a death of self. For this we need companions. If our lament is ever to lead to redemptive joy, we need assistance to weather the suffering required. No one is meant to go it alone, after all.

At the point of acceptance, the pain we feel doesn't go away, but it is hemmed with peace, laced with hope for the future. Here, hope articulates the lament of grief and loss, in the process birthing desire and creative action. Creative action is full of purpose and well-worth the pain. But if we are to nurture this creative seed to harvest, you and I must clarify our motive before we go much further.

If your motive is driven by fear—fear of pain, disapproval, missing out on pleasure, or not performing well enough—your efforts will not be sustainable. Planting our lament in fear is like sowing seed in a desert. Eventually, what you plant will wither and die at the root.

But plant your creative seed in the rich, dark, well-watered soil of joy and your crops will flourish.

Connected, creative makers feel things deeply and fully. They value their emotions and take note of what is happening within—*especially when they are afraid of what's inside*. That is why we must hack through the emotional jungle to get to hope-filled joy—joy must underlie any creative effort we make. That means, lest we grow bitter with festering grief, you and I must look for God in our circumstances, whether atypical or mundane. Moses, for example, may have seen many burning bushes in his life, as it is not unusual for vegetation beneath a blistering desert sun to self-combust. But he was paying attention. He looked closer and heard God's voice loud and clear.

We must listen to what God has to say, look at the redemptive invitation our grief holds, and notice what is going on around us. Questions like:

- Does the Bible say anything about the grief you feel? How does it lead you to believe this issue is important to God?

- Define the hope that surrounds the lament you are voicing. What would it look like if God redeemed your lament? How does your creativity lend itself to that vision?
- What purpose does this point you toward?
- How is God already at work around your lament? In response, how can you creatively join Him?
- How would your response and subsequent action make the kingdom visible and attractive? Would your efforts lead to deeper spiritual connection, authentic community, and God's glory? (Imagine the whole picture.)
- Do others around you discern this as part of your calling to God's Great—and creative—Commission? (Matthew 28:16–20)

My call to creative action centers on trumpeting God's creative presence and purpose for each of us. In these places, He meets us to create joy from sorrow, beauty from ashes, strength from oppression, peace from fear. He shows us everywhere! Vocationally, you may encounter Him in the sphere of social justice, politics, business, media, the arts, church, medicine, education, and so on. But for each of us the commission is to creative action, beginning with a cry of lament deep in our souls.

God knows what breaks our hearts, perhaps he is even using it to draw us closer to His. Whatever the case, God's intentions are good, and He will repair us. Through pain, God speaks into your being. To establish the heart of God as relevant and radiant in our time, you and I must champion one another. We encourage one another as we recognize and call out the unique creativity we see. Recognizing it, we bring hope as we speak to the precious kernel of identity that longs to grow from our lives. That is joy-full living. What better point in history for it, eh?

My friend Kent is a pastor in Southern California. He looks like a skinny surfing Santa, with eyes that dance, a heart that serves as a warm, refuge for creative leaders. As for Kent's kingdom vision, it's 20/20!

On the third Thursday of every month, Kent invites me and a group of 8 (-ish) other creatives to join him on Zoom for a discussion about our hearts and our art. He shares his own with us, too. Part of the time, we pray —listening on behalf of one another for the Lord's guidance and insight. Typically, as the call ends we share a swell of prophetic encouragement. A caring community can help us see things more clearly, you know? My prayer is that you have such robust spiritual friends in your life—friends who are faithful to draw you out of painful places with hope, and cheer for you in all your endeavors.

Committed companions.

One of our greatest existential fears is that we are ultimately alone. Yet that is a lie. God is delighted to be with you and me as we come to terms with the seed of our lament. Hardships and hurts may lead us to want to isolate, but you and I can't experience a joyful, fulfilling life by ourselves. God didn't make anybody that way. Our body, mind, and soul are all created to thrive together in community.

To God's and other's delight, your creative action is vitally important, as well. His purpose requires your unique creative energies, my friend. Whatever you do, let the joy of connecting with Him and others plow the soil ahead to prep it for sowing. And once you are able to voice that lament of yours, be sure to take off your shoes. Appreciate the soft-tilled earth beneath your feet. This field He cultivates for your creative action is holy ground, and it's finally planting season.

MAKER'S AFFIRMATION

Makers care deeply about the redemptive needs of the world that cause their soul to grieve—they make as a compassionate expression of their care for others.

I am a maker.

Maker Exercises

QUIETING

A habit of quieting helps to calm your central nervous system—moving you from a state of arousal to relaxation, lowering stress, and reducing anxiety.

- Immanuel, God, is with us.
- Quiet to connect with God's breath in your lungs.
- Use the first song on the chapter playlist ("Aftermath" by King and Country) or set a timer for four minutes.
- In a comfortable position—sitting with feet on the floor and hands in your lap or lying down with hands gently resting by your side—close your eyes and invite Jesus to quiet with you. Breathe deeply. Take air in through your nose as slowly as possible, letting your belly expand until your breath is full. Pause. Then breathe out until there is nothing left in your lungs. Pause again before your next inhalation.
- Repeat until the song or timer ends.

Then, take a minute to notice how you feel—emotionally and physically—before you move on—mentally note these feelings or sensations. (If you need help finding the right words, check out the list of feeling words in the Appendix.)

GRATITUDE

Start a Gratitude List by thinking of one thing you are thankful for right now. With eyes closed, vividly picture that person, place, or thing in your mind. Relax and breathe deeply as you appreciate every detail. Ask the Lord how he feels about who or what you are thankful for. Fully enjoy the memory.

When you feel the time is complete, write the detail in a journal or notebook. We will add to this throughout the book.

REFLECTION

1. Read Romans 8:18–28.
2. In your opinion, why are so many of us afraid of grief?
3. Does the Bible say anything about the grief you carry? How does it lead you to believe this issue is important to God?
4. Define the hope that surrounds your lament. What would it look like if God redeemed your lament? Consider how God is already at work around the situation. Is He inviting you to join Him? How does your creativity lend itself to that vision?
5. How would your action make the kingdom visible and attractive? Would your efforts lead to deeper spiritual connection, authentic community, and God's glory? (Imagine the whole picture.)

MAKER'S PROMPT

Make something to express your prayerful vision of the loving change you long to see.

Visio Divina

FOR CHAPTER 2

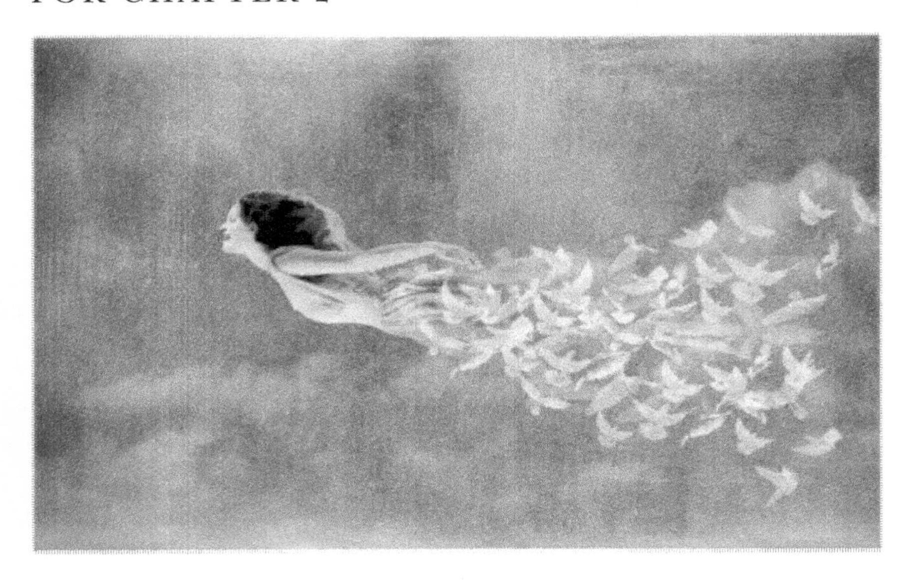

Julie McKnight, *Soaring Soul* (2021), composite digital art, Victor, Idaho.

READ.

Read the following verses aloud to discover their meaning.

> After He was baptized, Jesus came up immediately from the water; and behold, the heavens were opened, and he saw the Spirit of God descending as a dove and settling on Him, and behold, a voice from the heavens said, "This is My beloved Son, with whom I am well pleased."
>
> **MATTHEW 6:16–17 (NASB)**

REFLECT.

Read the verses again, circling any words or phrases that jump out at you.

Take time to consider: How is this passage speaking to me, today?

REIMAGINE.

When you're ready, turn your attention to "Soaring Soul" by Julie McKnight. Consider the passage in the context of the painting. Ask the Lord to guide your reimagining.

- What do you notice? (Consider the whole composition, mood, and any feelings it evokes)?
- Keep looking as you ask the Lord to help you see with His eyes. What comes to your attention? What stirs?

RESPOND.

Do you feel God inspiring you to any new creative depth or action? Describe your feelings and impressions. Thank Him for His word to you.

CHAPTER 2

WHY CREATIVITY MATTERS

"Make friends with the artist.
Let him rip off the veils of habit that obscure the beauty of Christ
in the faces we look at day after day. Let her restore color and texture and smell
to the salvation that has become disembodied in a fog of abstraction."
– EUGENE PETERSON,
FOR THE BEAUTY OF THE CHURCH

It was mid-June in the Ozarks. At midnight, I sat on the lakeside porch of my camp cabin, writing. Laced with hickory and dogwood, the musky summer air hung heavily across the lake, atop an Ozark Mountain, a light shone, all night, every night. Mysteriously, I was drawn to it.

I was fifteen and had been a camper for the past three summers. I had mastered the art of quietly padding my way to the screen door and ever-so-carefully opening it at just the right speed so the spring wouldn't make noise. Most nights, long after lights out and against all the rules, you could find me on the porch with a flashlight, my journal, a Bible, and a pen and pencil.

Perched on the porch with my provisions high up on a mountain overlooking Table Rock Lake, I was fascinated by the golden glow of the steady light across the valley and its dance on the silvery water between us.

It was like sneaking out to meet a crush. Hearing the crunch of the night watchman's footsteps patrolling the pea gravel path through the cabins, I got good at muffling my flashlight and leaning into the shadows, still as a mouse, until he passed. If anything, the risk made my hidden, post-midnight moments with God even more delicious. It was just our little secret —and it was only just the start.

On that porch, I felt the sacred light of God's steady presence calling me. Together we would talk about the day, write poems and prayers. I'd listen to his responses in Scripture, and sketch somewhat mystical metaphors for what the Holy Spirit revealed to my heart. Despite the long, sticky-hot, and rigorous camp days, something about that light was magnetic—and the time with God proved more important to me than sleep.

Going back over the pages of my camp journal as an adult, it is as if time has stood still. I'm right back on the porch, mesmerized by God's light across the water and the rich conversations between my heart and His. Little did I know then that what I was experiencing was God's creative wooing.

> In the beginning was the Word, and the Word was with God, and the Word was God. He was with God in the beginning. Through him all things were made; without him nothing was made that has been made. In him was life, and that life was the light of all mankind. The light shines in the darkness, and the darkness has not overcome it.
>
> **JOHN 1:1–3 (NIV)**

I was made to be a maker like Him. I sensed it, somehow—knowing before I *knew*. And, somehow, I know you are a maker too.

What "Creative" Does *Not* Mean

I've found the word "creative" to be a tricky one. Almost always when I ask people to define "creative," they shift uncomfortably and answer with a qualifying preamble like,

"Hmmm. That's a hard question." People fly by the seat of their pants when they try to define it-- especially if they don't see themselves as creative.

The consensus seems to be that to "be creative" is an act or an ability given to a lucky few, the gifted ones among us. Not only is this concept wrong, but it's also self- limiting, biblically inaccurate, and spiritually curbing (and that makes it exponentially wrong!)

For believers, the truth is that to be creative is to notice, acknowledge and nurture that part of the Holy Spirit in us and others. It is both a statement about our being, and a *way* of being. Being creative isn't a matter of self-sufficiency, it is a matter of soul-dependency—we are designed to live connected, purposeful lives.

A lot has been written and studied in recent years regarding creative process and creativity in general, so I want to be clear how *I* am defining the word: never is it a programmed outcome. Outcomes are soulless.

While I believe there is a place for design thinking and creative critique, business schools and marketers approach creativity as something that yields a "product." For something to be labeled "creative" in these tribes, by definition it must be new, novel, or otherwise unique. But the focus on product and function come at our expense. The importance of buzz-worthy results and high-dollar value assigned by many corporate cultures, social media influencers, and even some art institutions demean the treasure of what I define as being creative.

In their context, there may be a place for this—but this is not in the spiritual realm that I want us to dip a brush into.

Assigning processes, product goals, and program-driven objectives to creativity may fit functionally, but not spiritually.

Spiritually, do you see how this underestimates our creative identity? None of us fully recognizes the scope of our innate creative character. Our poor, bifurcated souls attest to it.

When we buy into believing that creativity is something we can wrangle, price, and control for our own productive purposes, don't we demean the treasure? You get what you pay for, I guess. If we allow ourselves to "price" our creative nature so low, we've been duped —and I think the enemy of our souls knows this.

As those made in the image of the Trinity, it is time for us to raise the bidding.

Engaging Imagination

The creativity that I'm talking about is a way of engaging life—a matter of character and rightful identity—and it is the treasure of everyday opportunities led by the Spirit. As creative people, you and I are hold space for Jesus. With heavenly endorsement, we lead lives marked by empowered presence, empathy, and holy-rooted identity. We have stories to tell. Until Christ returns, this world is ours to occupy—and to creatively multiply what we've been given (Luke 9:11–26).

So we don't waste any time, you and I have an opportunity to capture the collective imagination of the culture around us—to expect and affirm wonder, every day. Stepping into our authentic creativity, we extend a compelling invitation to others. God's grace gets traction. (After all, he didn't leave us with our "talents" expecting to come back to what he'd left. We are where we are to invest for Him!) The currency of His kingdom multiplies exponentially in the myriad ways we joyfully relate and grow with those around us.

An example: What does tap dancing have to do with capturing wonder and imagination?

Ask Andrew Nemr. Thanks to social media (words I never thought I'd say), I recently came across an internationally known tap dance artist and storyteller. In one of his TED Talks he tells the story of his life and how dance helped him integrate his thoughts, feelings, and—ultimately—his beliefs. Andrew describes how his full-life burnout led him to Dallas Willard's Four Great Questions of Life.

Through rhythm, dance, and story he captured my imagination in profoundly creative and novel ways—opening my mind and soul to consider the questions afresh: What is real? What is a good life? Who is a really good person? And how does one become a really good person?

Motivations and Values

From the beginning, God has invited us to an eternal creativity that is deeper, wider, and much higher than we realize. The desire for it resides in our heart of hearts—haunting all who long for more. Intuiting a better, more engaging way of purposeful life with God but seeing no clear Christian path, some give up searching for it. Like me, they figure those creative interactions with God—like my moments on the porch—are just quirky, private ways to enjoy God. They are sure they will snap out of it someday and find satisfaction in the more "serious" ways of engaging with God attained by traditionally religious folks. What they don't realize is that many of the "traditionally religious" folk they look up to aren't satisfied at all!

Just like my stint at the children's table, creatively speaking, we have learned to settle for less if we lean heavily on:

- What we know
- Doing things right

- Perfect efforts
- Fixing what is broken
- Controlling outcomes
- Brokering our power and talent
- Placing rules and theory (especially twisted Scripture) above actual practice
- Appearing strong on the outside
- Keeping people happy

Sadly, these methods and motives are the mark of people who have sold-out their souls (and I don't mean to God). A desire for certainty has displaced faith. We can't cast blame, though. All too typically, this approach is the best their spiritual landscape has offered. This is just "how it's done," religiously speaking. Perhaps, some of us rationally chalk our stifled yearnings and vulnerabilities up to "living on this side of heaven?"

Whatever the case, something causes the shine to fade from a vision of life with God—and that is a tragedy. You and I cannot flourish when the gifts of our relational, right brain are ignored. When we lose or subvert connection with God and others, you and I miss the whole point of life in Christ.

I'm not judging, here. We all learn to do our best with what we have been taught. But what if what we have been taught is grossly incomplete? What if the religion we have been taught has been working against the art of our becoming like Christ? Where is this evident in our lives and communities?

Creator Created

The creative part of our brain is initially sparked on the right side. On a variety of levels, something captures our attention. When we ignore the creative part of our being—settling for a mundane vision of life—we also ignore the *first* aspect of God's character introduced to us at the opening of the Old Testament. This is where we read: "In the beginning God created..." (Genesis 1:1).

For you and me to step into our truest selves, we've got to look into that mirror and recognize who is gazing back. Peeking at ourselves through His Word, the face of our God- given creativity greets us all.

We are stamped with the mark of the Creator, created *by* Him to create *like* Him. We are makers! Joyfully unique creative potential is built into each of us. Once unveiled, it is the key to transcendent awareness of God in all things, as well as motivation and lasting spiritual transformation. This transformation not only fuels our sense of significance but also expands God's glory in (and to) the world! Several days into God's world-making, He got around to making people: "Then God said, 'Let us make mankind *in our image*, in our likeness, so that they may rule'" (Genesis 1:26 NIV, emphasis added).

Everything God created says something about our Creator. But humankind uniquely bears the *imago dei* (image of God). Furthermore, we bear the image of the Trinity: Father, Son, and Holy Spirit.

The full potential of our identity—and the potential of the creative community—is undeniable. Please don't miss this: I'm not talking about embracing creativity as some kind of self-actualization technique. It is far more important than that. Embracing your creativity in all its forms is a matter of our soul's integration.

The first thing God did was go on a creative binge. If that's not a values statement, I don't know what is.

God didn't saddle us with the work of creating the world, but He *did* invite Adam and Eve into His creative process, encouraging them to name animals, to be fruitful, to play in the garden and to multiply (Genesis

1:28). Today, God continues to invite us to collaborate creatively with Him; embracing a kind of whole-brain, whole-life holiness in lifestyle of total engagement. Living with both right and left hemispheres engaged is a step toward the integration He has whispered throughout my life. My guess is you will begin to hear it, too—that is, if you haven't already.

Longing for Creative Integration

I am not alone in my longing to experience creative spiritual transformation. Years spent in the creative relational space—plus a decade working around thought leaders in spiritual formation—have convinced me of this.

Let me tell you about a young man named Eric who—like me—longed to integrate his creativity with the spiritual practice of ministry.

I had been invited by a seminary to speak during chapel. After my presentation, students lined up to ask questions. I noticed a young man in line nervously shifting his athletic frame from one foot to the other. When he got to the front of the line, his eyes welled with heavy tears. He pulled out his phone to show me a striking portfolio of artwork.

"I did this all before I was saved," Eric confessed, as though his art was an illegal substance. "But I don't do it anymore. I thought I had to choose. You can tell from my paintings that life was a little dark back then. I put it away because I didn't see how to make it part of my spiritual life—let alone my ministry. When I felt called to go to seminary, I figured I had to make the choice between my ministry and my art. I didn't think there was a place for my art in seminary."

I sensed that he had been carrying this for years.

"You read my mail when you talked about feeling as if you were at the children's table," he continued. "And that's been really painful. I've been wanting permission from somebody to integrate my creative side for a while, but every time I tried, I felt conflicted. I didn't hear God's clear invitation. Thanks for helping me see that my creative side isn't something I need to cut- off."

Maybe you've felt like Eric and me, too. For lack of community context, you've got vibrant creative ways of connecting with God that you have privatized. You consider these hidden, personal, and somehow, less important than the clearly religious activity you've witnessed around you. You may feel like an oddball for practicing your faith the way you do, but trust me, you're not alone! Followers in Jesus' day were equally confused by the religion that was modeled for them. To this day, in Orthodox traditions of Christianity the creative, logical, and spiritual cannot be excised.

Collaborating with God, we name, connect, represent imparted symbols, and help point one another in the direction of our true and transformed identity. If you and I don't wipe the fog from the mirror of His Word that has settled in the visage of our creative ways of being, we may miss the kingdom point. Tending to our expressive, relational side helps us notice when we've lost the joy of connection with another (God included). To the extent we pay attention and maintain an awareness of our joy, we will experience uninterrupted spiritual growth.

Our making is what generates our ever-growing joy! For Eric and me (and hopefully for you, too!) the best news is that we don't have to choose. We simply need to integrate our joyful identity with our extraordinary, logical abilities. By virtue of Western culture, we have already learned most of *how* this is done. *How* is what we know about our gifts and skills.

What too many are not yet convinced of is how essential our creativity is to our spirituality. When we value and feed the creativity of our relational being, we grow, becoming more and more like our Maker. By sharing our journey with other people, we help them recognize what these experiences really are: God-encounters. And in doing so, they may find themselves reconsidering what spiritual life and spiritual experiences are all about. By enlarging their perspective on what it means to connect creatively with God, perhaps they will be inspired to make something new with God.

We are meant to grow in complete ways, not with our creative self simply tacked on as an afterthought. After all, creativity is found in the very *beginning* of God's story! And, as we are made in God's image, it is in the beginning of our story too. Our story begins with His creative spirit imparted to us all—whether we recognize it or not, whether we love Jesus or not. Acknowledging the importance of this spark encourages us to shine our creative light. And the world is better for it!

So keep an eye out for the shine in you, and the shine others carry. Just as I was drawn by a light across the lake, your creative light is magnetic to those whose own light has been dimmed by a more cognitive approach to religion. It matters that much, dear maker.

MAKER'S AFFIRMATION

Makers value their experiences, feelings, intuition, and emotions as essential fodder for their creative life with God. This awareness cracks open their souls to make room for His redemptive work.

I am a maker.

Maker Exercises

QUIETING

Yawning dulls the activity of the sympathetic nervous system, signaling your parasympathetic nervous system that it is time to "rest and digest." Even if you aren't tired and it is nowhere near bedtime, make yourself yawn three times to quiet your body—and reset a balanced shalom state in your nervous system.

GRATITUDE

Think about a favorite memory of something creative you've done that made your heart soar. Close your eyes and thoroughly revisit the experience—with all your senses. When you were doing it, how did it feel physically? What emotions do you recall? Was anyone else part of the memory-making? What most delighted you about the endeavor? Write down the details of this memory on your Gratitude List.

End by thanking God for the experience.

REFLECTION

The book discussed the need for a colorful picture of vibrant kingdom life to guide us. Take some time to color yours in by reflecting on where you are:

1. Other than getting a ticket to heaven, what motivates your spiritual journey?
2. Do you know any lukewarm Christians? How would you describe their way of being?
3. How would my life change if Jesus were my first and most shining love?
4. Is your creative being part of your life with God? Does it influence your connection with others?
5. Are you living a whole-brained life with God or a linear, left-brained-only faith?
6. Read Genesis 1:1–3 slowly a few times. Take a few minutes and imagine the scene. What does this tell you about how God feels about creativity? Does anything make you curious?

MAKER'S PROMPT

Using the medium of your choice, make something that captures what you feel right now. Share your creation with someone and tell them why you made it—include feeling words in the story you tell.

Visio Divina

FOR CHAPTER 3

Carol Aust, *Breaking Bread* (2021), acrylic on canvas, Oakland, California.

READ.

Read through the Scripture below slowly, three times.

> "A new command I give you: Love one another. As I have loved you, so you must love one another. By this everyone will know that you are my disciples, if you love one another."
>
> **JOHN 13:34–35 (NIV)**

REFLECT.

Pay close attention to the words or phrases you connect with as you read. Circle them and write down any thoughts or feelings.

REIMAGINE.

Oakland artist, Carol Aust, paints paintings that tell personal stories—not necessarily hers, but those in our hearts. Invite the Lord to help you engage with her image, "Breaking Bread" and the Scripture reading as you contemplate the following:

- Consider the scene. What catches your attention, first?
- What story is it telling you?
- Where does the composition take you in your heart and mind?
- Do you sense any physical reaction to the scene?
- What does God have to say about these places in you?
- Does the painting capture a picture of your experience as a disciple of Jesus?—of His Church?

RESPOND.

What gesture of hospitality do you feel led to offer others?

CHAPTER 3

ATTACHMENT AND THE ROAD TO GREECE

"We can no more be formed in the image of Christ outside of corporate spirituality than a coal can continue to burn bright outside of the fire."
– ROBERT MULHOLLAND, *INVITATION TO A JOURNEY*

For our first grandchild's birth, I was blessed to be invited into the delivery room. During the height of the COVID pandemic, becoming a birth doula guaranteed me a place in the room to offer comfort and support, so I went through the intensive training to make it happen.

As Judah McCoy's mama and daddy will tell you, it was an arduous labor (hence the term) but at 2:17 a.m. that sweet baby made his entrance into the world just as the chorus of Kari Jobe's "The Blessing" crescendoed in the background. In the same moment, it was breathtaking, tear-spilling, and life-giving. Laid bare on my daughter's belly as the nurses did their things, Judah slowly began what is known in doula world as a breast crawl toward the faces, voices, and food source he desired most in the world. What a miracle in itself! May my heart never outgrow the joy of those first golden minutes of his life.

From the beginning, each of us is attached to our mother. Blood and bone are formed and fed by a connection with her and when we are birthed into this world, we look for her or whomever will help to provide for our basic needs (food, shelter, comfort, safety). We learn our value based on how well we attach and can depend on her (or other significant caregivers).

These foundations of attachment theory set our course, creatively and otherwise.

Though this drive evolves as we mature, the same motivation never really goes away.

God planted in our soul's a deep need to be seen, heard, protected, and cared for by dear others. "We are all looking for someone looking for us," says neurotheologist Dr. Jim Wilder. Within these relationships, we experience joy—the delight of being together. Our brains are organized around making that a reality.

As our source of life, it makes sense that God designed our relational attachment to Him as central to our spiritual journey, too. It is the beginning.

Who Do You Love?

When I was in first grade, I met Jesus. That year, my Sunday school teacher gave each of us in her class a groovy Bible translation, called *The Way*. It was the '70s, and the Bible included lots of images of joyful, Partridge family-esque young people out in the hip, Jesus-loving world.

The Jesus Movement was on fire and this translation burned around the world right along with it.

I loved that Bible and my teacher, Mrs. Thomlinson. She said if we would read our Bible, we could keep it. Do you know what I did? I read it of course! And, as I went, I would embellish its pages with the beautiful colors of my magically scented markers. (My favorites were lavender/ cotton candy, light yellow/banana, pink/ bubble gum, and green/mint.) Looking back, I honestly wonder which motivated me more—my love for God's Word, my teacher, or those markers. Whatever the case, it got me started creatively connecting my faith with art early on.

Coloring, naming, reflecting, connecting, making meaning around Jesus and His Word inspired me to know Him better. Developing healthy habits of relating with Him spills over to the rest of our life and relationships. Over time, a general awareness gives way to trust through these bonds—our capacity to attune with God and others grows. We develop a sense of identity.

As a matter of spiritual formation and attachment theory, it is a fact: who (or what) we love profoundly impacts who we become. When our basic attachment needs for comfort and security are met, we are free to explore the world with boldness, curiosity, and joy. This confidence helps us experience better connection with others (God included). The importance of secure attachment cannot be overstated because our earliest connections shape us—sticking with us for life! The more these bonds are reinforced, the stronger they become. Ultimately, they define our character and identity.

The same holds true for those who experience what is known as "insecure attachment." Their varying ability to attach shapes their identify and character. Depending on your research source, upward of 60 percent of people fall into this category.

When secure attachment is missing, the negative effect on our spiritual growth is huge. In our minds, this should underscore the need for healthy, creative connection with others. Anyone who feels alone and afraid will shut down—emotionally, spiritually, and intellectually. This affects our relationships and capacity to mature, creating negative consequences in the formation of character.

To a certain extent, our relationships dictate our life experiences. If you or I struggle with insecure attachment, our identity may get stuck in a swirl of emotional conflict—unable to integrate right-brain relational impulses with appropriate left-brain action. As a result, we can find ourselves acting out or faking it, pretending on the outside that everything is okay when that is far from the truth. There is nothing more important to our health and well-being—spiritually, mentally, emotionally, and physically—than the experience of secure (unconditional, comforting) attachment relationships. (For more information, see the Appendix).

The rules of attachment apply to our spiritual growth and transformation, too—we become like who (Jesus) we love most. So, who—or what—do you love most? Honest answers to this essential question expose our attachments—good *and* bad, reveal our hidden motivations, and can bring even our subtlest addictions to light.

Something Is Missing

Many Western church circles have similar definitions for spiritual formation and transformation. One I especially like is from pastor and author Ruth Haley Barton's *Life Together in Community: Experiencing Transformation in Community*: "Spiritual transformation is the process by which Christ is formed in us—for the glory of God, for the abundance of our own lives and for the sake of others" (see Galatians 4:19, Romans 8:29, and Romans 12:1–2)." These words are rich with meaning, making it clear that our spiritual formation and transformation is a process—not a program or a product.

Yet what remains fuzzy with it and other widely accepted definitions is the necessary role of relationships and community in that process—and more importantly, how to build and maintain relationships, so you and I are able to mature relationally. We've all heard the saying: Christianity isn't a religion, it is a relationship." So why the heavy emphasis on facts surrounding the former?

Spiritual information alone never resulted in anyone's transformation.

Years in the field and countless studies have verified that spiritual transformation cannot happen apart from a robust combination of Scripture *and* community. Yet, until I met Dr. Jim Wilder in 2007, it never occurred to me how my spiritual "education" had not provided practical tools, experiences, or information about emotional and relational growth as part of the mix. As soon as I heard Jim's teaching in 2007, it spun me around! ***This*** *is what has been missing*, I thought. ***This*** *changes everything about how people are being taught to grow spiritually!* To the 60 (plus) percent who are insecurely attached, surely such insight would strengthen their walk with God, too.

A Lonely Trip

One of my closest friends from middle school is Greek—100 percent, pass the baklava and pour me some ouzo, Greek. Stern Uncle Petros, hilarious Aunt Sondra, stunning Antigone, quiet little Georgios—so many characters! Her family is huge and lively. They cook for a week for Orthodox Easter (for those who don't know, it is the week after Protestant Easter). Although I didn't spend time with her close-knit extended family, through Ann's stories—and the fabulous leftovers of exotic dishes she brought over to my house—I fell in love with the culture. I particularly loved her descriptions of the incense-infused and iconic mystery of their Church services.

It all captured me.

Add a little scenery from *Mama Mia*—white stucco villages beside the crystal blue Aegean waters—and my fascination with Greek culture is complete. Decades later, I am still swept away by the idea of traveling to those islands. Though an invite would have been unlikely, I imagine it would have been especially fun to go with Ann and her boisterous family!

In fact, if someone bought me a lone ticket for a Grecian tour, I'd still be pretty excited. More than just the Mediterranean beauty and culture, the chance to see the places Scripture talks about with my own eyes? I wouldn't say no. Even though I'd prefer to travel with someone I know, I'm a sucker for an adventure.

Unless, however, you told me that I'd be traveling with a group of people who didn't want to know anything about me or let me know them, people who never laughed, never encouraged me, and didn't seem to care if I was on the trip (except if I carried their luggage or fetched their refreshments!). If this were the case, I would stop following them around. At a certain point, I'd begin to feel more like an unwanted guest, or a waiter with a rude table.

Honestly, it sounds too lonely, too rejecting, too frustrating. Especially on vacation, who wants to be used that way?! If people don't want to connect, I'm out. Each of us wants something *more.*

Even if we know and do all the right "Christian" things, it's not very satisfying, nor will it leave us transformed. (You and I have more than enough experience to tell us that.) We need to know and be known by God and a few close others for the trip to be meaningful and life changing.

On the journey to become like Jesus, that kind of true connection helps us travel well together. It is authentic, transparent, and reciprocal, making you and me willing to know and be known by one another. Sure, it takes vulnerability and can challenge us sometimes, but because deep connections are enjoyable and make us feel welcome, they yield joy for everyone on the trip.

Creativity in our relationship with Christ and others makes the adventure more fun and life-giving for each of us. In the process, we offer the best of ourselves back to God and to each other. When we do, an essential part of God's character shines through. By affirming what we see in one another, we embolden our true, Christlike identity. Rich, relational side-roads are the best part of the biblically-based map God has charted for our spiritual life. All of a sudden, appreciation for one another grows. Your ways inspire me to notice even more of God's wonder in the world—and hopefully I inspire you to do the same. Led heart-before-head, people intertwine with God's purposes and His Word.

Creative Connection and Discipleship

If we are going to invite people on a discipleship journey without taking time to appreciate them or revealing our own unique creativity, you and I are missing the point. We hide ourselves under a bushel, so to speak (Matthew 5:15). But when you and I come to terms with the unique dimensions of our own creativity we will enjoy life with God even more. It's like a permission slip. Suddenly, we realize that these people, places, and things that bring us joy help us know and trust Him more. The resulting spiritual connection makes us *real.*

Bushel basket removed, vibrant life revealed.

Experiencing and expressing our creativity exposes the warmth of God's fire and invites others near. Our souls crack open to others as we communicate, validate, and comfort them with the gifts, skills, and joys we have been given. See? The art of our Spirit-led lives puts off a glow that invites people to connect. And as our glow gains His strength, Jesus shines.

Doing the Christian life otherwise is a lot like inviting someone on the solo trip I described before. They sign up for what they think will be the ultimate destination by way of a memorable tour only to find no one is interested in having them along. They return home empty.

When you and I don't purposefully delight in one another we make others invisible, in a sense. Our relational connection has been such an afterthought all this time, we leave scores of opportunities to connect and understand each other on the table. Limiting our church relationships to functional familiarity limits how much we enjoy and appreciate one another—and it shows.

In these times, it seems more important than ever.

Make Room for the Makers

Religion like this crowds-out God's plan and distances people from Him. Today, we talk a good game about things like personal relationship with Jesus, and community with other believers but seem to have missed the point: Jesus offered us a vibrant life with Him. A vibrant life is a creative life. Extending the same to one another is a natural part of growing to be more like Him.

It's widely accepted that "artists" carry the gift of inspiration, vision, imagination, intuition, passion, and the like. But what about people who aren't full-time artists? What about you? What about those you love and influence? It is no small thing to consider. You have a creative life. Letting it show reveals who you are to me and others. It helps us build relationship and appreciation between us. Relationships matter because connection leads to joy and the joy center of your brain. Our encouragement of each other matters too.

So, a few questions:

- So how and when do you feel God's presence most readily?
- Are you and I living lives that invite people to draw near to —to join in the party with the God we love?
- Are we "doing church" in a way that demolishes hierarchy and welcomes everyone—all of their creative selves —to show up?

- Are we offering reciprocal relationship with God, and one another? —or are we handing them a scroll?
- How have you let your "art form" be known in your faith community?
- One way requires creativity, the other does not.

Combined with Scripture, Christ-centered relationships promise sustainable transformation. By itself, knowledge alone does not, and spiritual practices cannot.

Developing creative character and identity.

We need one another to fully know ourselves. People sense when they are seen, heard, and known when we indicate that we see, hear, and know them. If you and I really plan to fulfill the call to make disciples, we can't ignore this kind of "getting personal." The need to nurture healthy attachment in our lives is inescapable.

Study after study proves that positive spiritual growth and maturity is not sustainable apart from relationships. Though biblical study is central to all aspects of discipleship, reading your Bible doesn't lead to transformation, either. Neither can a privatized, solo-style faith. You and I authentically animate Jesus by what lights us up and how we care for one another.

Sharing our whole selves is how we come to know and be known. It takes time and vulnerability—and it is how our longing to be seen becomes a sense of belonging. Opening up about what lights us up—fully accepting and enjoying who we are—serves as a model and invites others to do the same. In the journey toward bearing His image, this extends unconditional lovingkindness and helps the Word become flesh in our lives. Hand-holders, cheerleaders, champions for the mutual good are joy-bringers in every way. Jesus wants fired-up followers. To be indifferent about the creative mark we are making is to be, well, apathetic—dare I say, lukewarm. Lukewarm is neither joyful nor peaceful. It is *meh*. The creative part of who you and I is never *meh*.

In case the idea throws you off, let me be clear: I'm not suggesting we need to pull out our Jesus paint-by-numbers kit at our next Bible study. What would be helpful, however, is to consider how our relationships and the content we are covering may lend to authentic, experiential encounter. On a practical level, let's ask ourselves: what creative way could I carry the thing God's been impressing on my spirit into the meetings I have ahead of me today? To small group this week?

Meeting Ryan

I met my friend Ryan at a conference just as I walked up to the registration table. Despite the crowds, his big smile and the loud, multicolored hat atop his tall frame made him hard to miss. In fact, his dress and manner were so bold, I figured he was part of the conference team.

He was talking to another facilitator which gave me yet another reason to believe he was on the payroll.

Yet, nothing could have been further from the truth. Just like me, he was a conference attendee. Also, just like me, Ryan was fascinated with the concept of joy. For Ryan, the big question is how the majority of Jesus followers overlooked its significance within their spiritual journey.

His hat got my attention, sure, but the heart and depth of Ryan's story—and the solid creative rationale behind it—is what held my gaze.

"Jesus is the best thing going!" he said with an enthusiastically wide grin. "So why aren't more Christians happy about that? We need to show people out there in the world our joy!" There was intense sincerity to his words.

Honestly, I was intrigued, and I could see this guy's good heart might be missed if people got distracted by his flamboyant tactics. Still, no one could deny Ryan was FUNNNN! with a capital "U" for unicorn (which is a-whole-nother story). By the time the week was over, I knew a whole lot more about what he meant.

Hosted by THRIVEtoday, the theme of the conference was on building exactly the relational skills that seem to be lacking in most of our spiritual formation journeys.

One night, I was leaving the conference hotel just as Ryan walked into the lobby. I kid you not, we stood there for two and a half hours as I probed, pushed, exhorted, and investigated his many stories and the motives behind his colorful, creative exterior.

I learned that Ryan came from a happy and successful upper-middleclass family in Chicago. From a young age, he was a party boy with a hilariously precocious streak, a generous heart, and a love for people. His grandma had told him about Jesus. Raised Catholic, he had a friend in college who had been a missionary to Thailand, and he knew a few Protestant Christians but that was it. He had only known the religious side of faith (not the relational). So, when his family "blew up" as the result of a divorce, so did his church attendance.

Ryan's stories left me slack-jawed. Like the story of how he met Jesus.

It all started with the breakup of a seven-year relationship that sent him on a drunken three-month, four country traveling binge. At the time, the trip seemed like a good idea—until he returned home and wanted to reconcile with his ex-girlfriend. Long story short, she said no. She was in love with someone else.

At that point, Ryan decided to visit his mom who had moved to Arizona following the divorce. She was worried about him. At that point, he was a little worried about himself. He was lost and sinking further into depression. While there, took a break from drinking. He also went with his mom to her new Lutheran church. Being a people person, Ryan met a few "nice but nerdy" guys who invited him to attend a young adults group, which he did a couple times heading back home to Chicago.

Feeling decidedly better, Ryan continued to stay on the wagon. At the invitation of a friend, he started going to the gym on a regular basis. Little did Ryan know that Little did Ryan know that his gym friend knew Jesus. That gym also became where Ryan ran into his college friend who was still a missionary in Thailand. Their "chance reunion" during her visit home eventually led to Ryan's prayer of commitment to Christ.

After accepting Jesus, Ryan still struggled. With the help of mentors and good counseling, he realized the church he had started attending was controlling, spiritually abusive, and more like a cult. At the same time, Ryan realized his work environment was controlling and toxic too. Even though he enjoyed a lucrative career, he quit his job and walked away from his church—trusting that God had something better for him.

To grow his faith, he dove into the Word, found a solid church, and continued meeting with mentors.

Hearing Ryan's story, it was easy to see how the Lord had been seeding Ryan's search for joy. In fact, his longing for joy began to shape his choices. Before long, he began to offer people experiences of relational joy and connection. For an entire year, he kept a list of people's birthdays and phone numbers and called over 1,000 people on their special day to let them know he was thinking of them. Ryan began cooking for people, developed his "unrivaled" woodfired pizza recipe, became an Airbnb host of three properties, installed an ice cream cooler at his house, and began hosting an annual Christmas party for 100 people.

He discovered that gathering friends and strangers together, blessing others, and giving people an opportunity to make joyful memories afforded him the chance to encourage and authentically connect with them. In the process, Ryan saw how God worked through ripples of joy (which happens to be the name of his YouTube channel).

As we stood talking in the hotel lobby, he told me that if these things give him a chance to organically talk about Jesus, that was great—but it is not imperative.

Short version: it wasn't hard to see I was dealing with a wildly joyful, creative, and genuine soul. Like so many creatives, Ryan needed to be (1) delighted in for his uniqueness, (2) encouraged for his obedience, and (3) dreamed alongside.

Later he shared with me that our conversation was the first time someone had so quickly understood, called out, seen him. He was drawn to my curiosity and the way I put words around his creativity. The fact that I was honestly excited by what God was up to in his life gave Ryan permission to share more freely and to a new depth.

For me, the conversation was riveting. For Ryan? These spiritual practices became more than a quirky, private venture. He said talking with me helped him harness his passion and affirmed that what he'd been hearing from God wasn't crazy. Our chance meeting in the lobby created an inspiring opportunity for each of us to talk about who we love most (Jesus) and the creative impact this joyful attachment is having on who we are becoming!

In my soul, the discussion deeply underscored the reality of creating joy as a means of connecting with God and others. The following Scripture captures what I'm getting at: "And let us consider how we may spur one another on toward love and good deeds, not giving up meeting together, as some are in the habit of doing, but encouraging one another—and all the more as you see the day approaching." (Hebrews 10:24–25, NIV). Especially in recent years, does this describe *your* church experience? If not, consider this a permission slip to find Jesus-centered fellowship that does.

This "spurring" is just *part* of what our "artsy side" has to offer. You and I can creatively see, hear, know, and companion others like no boxed curriculum ever will. Engaged believers risk their creative souls for one another, probably because we know it is what we have longed for: belonging in this way.

Surrounded by brainiacs and good Bible teaching, I diminished my creative side for years.

All the signals and teaching I received led me to believe that my creative inclinations just weren't "as important" to the development of a solid (read, *intellectual*) Christian walk. That is on me. But as one who was highly invested and motivated in her own discipleship journey, let me be extremely clear: I think the body of Christ has the message backward, too. We have made knowing *about* God more important than knowing Him. And we've done the same to one another. Honestly, it keeps things more comfortable.

Caged Birds & Creative Freedom

Too much emphasis on intellect creates a cage of comparison, critique, and compromise for all things creative. Sure, the bird can still sing, but can it soar? No. Content for a long time, I never pushed on the cage door. I perched on the confines of traditional religious activities, engaged in spiritual disciplines, and socialized in faith-based circles—but it was lonely. A part of my soul had its wings clipped. When we remove creativity from the realm of spiritual practice, that is what happens. There is no place to live but the birdcage. For many able to keep their wings—encouraged in their gifting outside of Christian setting—as soon as the cage door cracks, they fly away for freer skies. These birds may get away with their faith intact but how sad for us all.

Embracing creativity as a spiritual practice renews parts of our soul, visible and invisible to others. We will see signs of it. Our thoughts, feelings, and character respond, making us more

- Engaged
- Energized
- Playful
- Humble
- Curious
- Joyful
- Empathetic
- Present
- Imaginative
- Supportive
- Grateful
- Kind
- Generous
- Passionate
- Gracious
- Responsive
- Authentic
- Other ____________

It's a way of life.

Acknowledged or not, creative connection is a need we all share — even the most introverted among us feel it. It is part of who we are, and it calls us heavenward! God made us for relationship with Him, as well as one another. Sharing oxygen in a same room (or church, or Bible study) isn't enough. After a while, it is bound to get stale.

Formation vs. Transformation

Individual efforts of spiritual formation—things like Bible study, spiritual disciplines, worship, serving—is a *part* of our transformation.

But it is relationships with God and other people that built the bridge to the soul integration for which we long. When healthy, it's where we all find healing.

For better or for worse, our important relationships change who we are and who we are becoming. In relationship with others, you and I cultivate the fruits of the Spirit described in Ephesians 5—love, joy, peace, patience, kindness, goodness, faithfulness, and self-control. Over-intellectualizing our faith is like introducing drought to these crops in our character. Without honest interaction with others, the harvest suffers.

If what I have to draw on is going to be adequate to form joyful Christian character, I need others. It begins when we become aware of what is going on in our hearts, souls, minds, and our relationships. Complete with all God's glorious creative potential within, our hearts yearn to be seen. We are seen and heard, known and accepted, worked and refined in relationships with the Lord and those He puts in our path.

From here, we learn to speak the soul language of others. For too long, I didn't know anyone else spoke mine. Neither did Ryan. Still, each of us held a tender confidence that we were to keep speaking, creating, and drawing others to the meaning our Maker had placed within our hearts.

Eventually, we meet others. They hear us. Seemingly seeing into our being, they call out our creativity and, slowly, as we come to believe they really mean what they say, trust develops between us. When that happens, it brings joy—partly because, odds are, we have underestimated the power of our creativity. If others can envision our creative value, the truth of it swells within us.

Gaining courage, we pursue our creative passions more boldly.

If we want to help one another become like Jesus, I need to see, hear, and learn from *you* and *your creative* language. That way, if and when either of us wander off, our collective vision can call us back to the dusty, vibrant life in the studio of our soul's transformation.

Creative space is a risky place to enter in the life of another person, but it is where we must venture together. Trust me, the rewards are rich.

MAKER'S AFFIRMATION

Makers share themselves deeply —connecting with God and others out of a desire to know them, be known, and to participate in the ongoing process of spiritual transformation.

I am a maker.

Maker Exercises

QUIETING

Play song #1 on this chapter's playlist, "Hand to Hold" by JJ Heller, as you hug someone you love. Hold the embrace without speaking. Notice how it feels in your body and mind. Remember to relax and breathe deeply. What "feeling words" would you use to describe the experience? (Remember to see the Appendix if you can't find the right feeling words.)

GRATITUDE

Who made you feel seen, heard, understood, and cared for this week? Looking back, remember what it felt like in your body. Describe what the person did that made you feel that way. Add this to your Gratitude List.

REFLECTION:

1. How and when do you feel God's presence most readily?
2. Are you and I living lives that invite people to draw near to —to join in the party with the God we love?
3. Are we "doing church" in a way that demolishes hierarchy and welcomes everyone—all of their creative selves —to show up?
4. Are we offering a reciprocal relationship with God and one another? —or are we handing them a scroll?
5. How have you let your "art form" be known in your faith community?

MAKER'S PROMPT

Make memories over a meal.

Hospitality is a spiritual discipline reflected in Scripture—preparing meals, accommodating travelers, cleaning homes, sharing fish, washing feet, anointing heads, etc.

Gathering friends or family together is a chance to bless them with authentic time to connect and make joyful memories. It effectively demonstrates grace and gratitude for others. Pick a random theme to make it fun. Let everyone take part by making it a potluck, or have everyone bring an ingredient for a big pot of chili or chicken tortilla soup. Over dinner, pose a question to be discussed (for example: what is the best news you got this week? Who or what made you feel special today? Describe why your best friend is so great?) After dinner, play games in teams. Go out of your way with simple, thoughtful touches that bless your guests with a sense that they've been safe, seen, heard, and welcome in this company of friends.

Visio Divina

FOR CHAPTER 4

Sue Shehan, *Bountiful* (2013), soft pastel on paper, Castle Pines, Colorado.

READ.

Read the Scripture below aloud.

> Oh yes, you shaped me first inside, then out;
> you formed me in my mother's womb.
> I thank you, High God—you're breathtaking!
> Body and soul, I am marvelously made!
> I worship in adoration—what a creation!
> You know me inside and out,
> you know every bone in my body;

You know exactly how I was made, bit by bit,
how I was sculpted from nothing into something.
Like an open book, you watched me grow from conception to birth;
all the stages of my life were spread out before you,
The days of my life all prepared
before I'd even lived one day.
PSALM 139:13–16 (MSG)

REFLECT.

As you read through it a couple more times, circle any phrases, word pictures, or words that stand out to you.

REIMAGINE.

Now, prayerfully consider the beautiful oil pastel, *Bountiful*, by artist Sue Shehan. She wonderfully captures the majesty, power, and mystery of a thunderhead over the plains in her work. Aren't clouds amazing? Just as God sculpts mist and vapor into clouds which have no real structure or substance, he forms us. He works from nothing to craft the awesome innerworkings of our body, mind, and soul to house His Spirit. (Visit AmyPierson.com to see the painting in color.)

Let the following questions guide your reflections on what God speaks to you through His Word and Sue's painting. Journal your responses:

- What are you drawn to in this landscape?
- What are you drawn to in Psalm 139 that the painting echoes? Does the scene capture any of the words or phrases you circled from the passage? Journal the details of your insights.

- What truth, hope, or encouragement is the Lord offering you?

RESPOND.

Quietly contemplate what you've received. Thank God for what He has creatively shared with you. Now, go outside, lie on a blanket, and watch the clouds drift by as you contemplate God's wonder.

CHAPTER 4

SKYDIVING THROUGH CLOUDS OF NEUROSCIENCE

"Making seems embedded in us from 'the beginning.' Such an impulse embeds our vision in actual earthly materials. So our journey to 'know' God requires not just ideas and information, but actual making, to translate our ideas into real objects and physical movements."
– MAKO FUJIMURA

I admit it. Math and I are not friends. It's not a new thing. The problem solidified for me in sixth-grade algebra. It didn't make sense on any level. And, my teacher, Mrs. X, who called me by my last name, seemed to take sickening delight in loudly mocking my errors in front of the class. I felt regularly humiliated the entire year. Clearly, I was not going to be able to solve for y (or why she did that) without someone's help. At that point, my math abilities became frozen in time. I embraced my deficiency, shrugging it off as if I didn't care. Oh, but I *did* care.

A part of me shut down. And that learning wound sticks with me to this day.

Now, anytime I am asked to run numbers in front of someone, it is as if my brain goes missing. My blood pressure and respiration anxiously spike, pushing my heart rate upward the longer I keep people waiting. I've learned to accommodate this weakness in my life (see tip calculator app, budget software, and husband's stellar math ability), but sometimes learning wounds aren't so easily addressed.

What about the walking *creative* wounded among us? The ones who have "learned" from the responses of others that they are "deficient" in creativity? Who, by inference or comparison, have adopted the idea that they "just aren't creative"?

One study of shame uncovered that 85 percent of us suffer learning wounds as children, and of that majority, *50 percent have a wound involving creativity.*[2] Apparently, there are a lot of us walking with a creative limp (or denying that we are limping, even though it is plain for everyone to see). Is it any wonder creative integration has not been widely considered as part and parcel of our spiritual transformation? But this is where our passions live.

Falling through the Clouds

Warning: This next bit may feel dizzying but hang in there. We are about to skydive through the mental clouds to take a 50,000-foot look at some brain science and the impact our attachments make.

Between misperceptions about our two hemispheres and considering how most of us began our walk with Jesus, you may be surprised by some of what this chapter explores. But take a deep breath, grab your ripcord, and let's jump!

The Left and Right Hemispheres and What They Do

Though it won't heal the wounds we have all suffered, understanding our design specs is important. Admittedly oversimplified, we will talk in essential terms of the left and right brain. (Even though, in reality, parts of the brain must work together—especially during the complex process of creating something.)

But for the most part, here are the functions of each side of the brain:

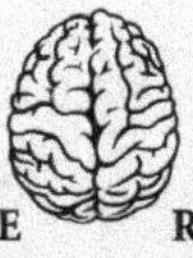

LEFT HEMISPHERE	RIGHT HEMISPHERE
Focusing on Parts	Looking at the Whole
Logic	Creativity
Linear Thinking	Relational Attachment
Learning	Assessing Situations, Feelings & Surroundings
Exploring	Awareness
Discovering	Emotional Attunement
Language	Synthesizing
Problem-Solving Explaining & Storytelling	Imagining
Strategizing	Intuiting
Choosing	Establishing Individual Identity
Analyzing & Identifying	Forging Group Identity

The **left hemisphere** of our brain is predominantly responsible for logical things like language, learning, decision-making, beliefs, problem-solving, and math. It is narrowly focused and task oriented. Concrete absolutes for logical procedures, actions and disciplines are executed here—and "it's science" (cue Nacho Libre). Left-brain actions shape our identity by helping us succeed in tasks like figuring out $\sqrt{58}$, learning how to drive, or discovering a cure for COVID.

The left brain is always responding to input. **Five times per second**, nerve impulses travel up the spinal cord to the base of the brainstem, continuing through the brain until they reach the left brain. As fast as that may seem, our left brain responds more slowly than the right.

The **right hemisphere** of our brain predominantly makes us aware of our needs, as well as physical, mental, and emotional sensations. It also oversees our intuition and relationships—the ways we connect and relate with others.

Before we are even conscious of it, this hemisphere can "read the room." Unclinically speaking, when it walks into a room, it quickly picks up nonverbals—the 80 percent of communication that includes unspoken moods and vibes. It then processes that information—cycling nerve impulses **six time each second**—far ahead of the logical, analytics of our left brain.

Right-brain emotions, experiences, and relationships shape our **identity** most powerfully. In fact, the joy-sensitive area where your identity lives is just behind your right eye in the cerebral orbital prefrontal cortex.

In other words, the right brain establishes our *way of being* in the world. It's the basis for connecting us to God and others that ultimately leads to the development of our character and identity. Seeing things broadly—as a whole—our right-brain functions of thought, emotions, and memories "talk" to us all the time, providing information. And, funny thing, so is God. Both necessitate a quiet shift of attention to become aware of what is being said.

Where to Begin

As soon as many of us "found God," we were very likely nudged in the direction of left hemispheric learning by established, more mature believers. We were told what scriptures we should study, what books to read, what spiritual disciplines to adopt, the "rules" we needed to follow, which Bible study to join, and so on. Each of these highly focused tasks land squarely in logical, left-brain procedures.

Even though these things are significant aspects of our life with God, they don't hold the key to lasting spiritual transformation. We can beef up our gray matter by acquiring more knowledge, but it won't form Christlike character. Can we learn from these disciplines? Sure. But in and of themselves, will these activities prove sustainable? Probably not. Sustainable spiritual growth happens when we purposefully integrate our relational, right-hemispheric ways into what we are learning and how we spend our time. (But have *we* ever been taught about *how* or *why* this is essential to discipleship?)

In their book *The Other Half of Church,* Dr. Jim Wilder and Michel Hendricks put it in a nutshell: The left brain runs at the speed of words; the right brain runs at the speed of joy.[3] Joy is a right-brain experience—and joy also forms and transforms our character. The awareness, attunement, and identity recognized in our right brain makes a difference in the quality of any left-brain action or experience that follows.

Within the field of neuroscience it is widely accepted that there are seven primary emotions that you and I experience. Joy, fear, anger, disgust, sadness, shame, and hopeless despair. Joy and fear are the two "biggies"—the buckets into which all other emotions (and their choice synonyms) fall. That is to say, there is only ONE neurologically recognized emotion which is positive (JOY). The other six emotions result from the primary emotion of fear.

In order to begin integrating both hemispheres, we need to learn how to pay attention to the information our right brain has to offer. You and I must become aware of the emotional energy, information, and senses that register in our right brain. Good or bad isn't the right question. Simply developing an ability to observe what is going on both in and around us—without judging it—helps cultivate healthy **awareness**. The best time to do this is before we take an action and find ourselves mindlessly following entrenched left-brain patterns. (Think: trigger.)

Slowing our pace a bit gives us an opportunity to notice what's *really* happening spiritually, emotionally, physically, and mentally. We are more present, aware of our inner landscape. Practiced this consistently and it becomes easier and more natural to do. Just like physical exercise, whatever you and I mindfully practice creates mental habits that strengthen connections in our brain resulting in lifelong change and growth. The fact that what we practice can form and change connections in our brain is known as neuroplasticity—and the growth of this white matter can happen our entire life long.

As we learn to live more rightly ordered, you and I become attuned—left and right brain meet in the "executive center" of ourselves. And when this happens, the impact on every area of our lives is huge.

This is the impact of our relationships.

By God's design, both hemispheres (the whole brain) work together to ultimately synchronize with those around us. In fact, our brain contains mirror neurons designed to connect and reflect the emotions of those around us. For example, when we are with people who are happy, sad, or excited, we tend to feel happy, sad, or excited with them. Together, we attune with each other—amplifying emotion and helping one another find identity.

Healthy relationships help you and me validate feelings, find comfort and reassurance that we are not alone, and repair hurts that may have happened along the way. (Marcus Warner, E. James Wilder. *Rare Leadership*) These form our capacity for empathy and attachment—these develop important relational skills, build relationships, and change who we are into who we are meant to be (identity).

When we lead with our left brain alone, you and I lose—forfeiting the opportunity to connect. We give up our true, spiritual identity—and this disconnect hampers our creative efforts. Making important space for awareness and attunement with self, God, and others empowers us for a dynamic, kingdom-now life.

Tangled in Left-brain Trees

Too often it seems a lot of us get in trouble—missing any right-brain target and tangled in left-brain trees like a misguided parachute. Let me explain.

Especially these days, you've probably noticed that handing someone a book or the key talking points of your educated opinion on a controversial cultural problem doesn't seem to be very effective these days (think race relations, COVID variants, masking, politics, no fly zones). *Of course*, you delivered your insight kindly, ever so diplomatically, certainly like Jesus would. Based on the tension in the room, you ascertain that the person you are addressing has probably written you off as clueless or narrow-minded. *The nerve.*

What is a thoughtful person to do?

I can tell you what we should *not do* (sadly and largely based on personal experience). We should not base our argument—especially our faith-tangent ones—on traditional left-brain functions. If we do, you and I will be fighting blind. Doing so is a set up. In that state, we won't have the awareness, emotional attunement, spiritual insight, and the necessary ability to connect with whomever we are talking to. And it shows!

Most of the time, we use our left brain to argue or build a good case to change the opposing view. Yet, James wrote, "My dear brothers and sisters, take note of this: Everyone should be quick to listen, slow to speak and slow to become angry, because human anger does not produce the righteousness that God desires" (James 1:19–20 NIV).

What James is describing requires us to use our right brain *first*! God knew this long before brain research and fMRI scans existed. (My guess is He flashed a wide grin when some grad student first uncovered this data in the lab.)

To live this way is going to take some retraining. When fear-based responses rule, so does our left-brained, emotionally unintelligent, unreflective side. Subverting our right hemisphere, we react in uninformed, logical processes. In those moments, you and I don't see the whole picture. And, as we've already said, you need your *whole* brain to respond in a holy appropriate way.

When our emotions are out of sorts and we are hunkered down in fear, our brain looks a lot like that of a heroin addict. We are unable to function at our creative and relational best. Plus, after we've been using our left brain to argue, fMRIs show a change in our brain that negatively effects our prayer life.

Dogged by Problems

Whether we realize it or not, when you and I fall into this trap, we are no longer fighting to be understood or to peacefully resolve an issue—we are fighting to win. The process becomes less interpersonal and winning becomes more important than our relationship with the other person. Within us, pride bristles, judgments bark. Joy and grace run away down the street as our negative emotions nip at their heels.

Our left-brain fails to integrate the necessary components between problems and relationships. As tensions flare, fear burrows further under the fence—cementing our "justified" position. Our reticular activating system effectively dismisses any stance that is not aligned with our own. We just can't connect—with ourselves or anyone else. We choose sides. We miss the unique, creative connections possible in such rare, raw moments. Divisions amplify in our body, mindset, and voice tone. When this is happening, what we really need to do is step back and settle down.

Means such as deep breathing, tapping, yawning, and stretching, seeking a hug also demonstrate great effects on lowering blood pressure, and slowing down our heart and respiration rates. In other words, simply pausing for a few minutes can help us physically quiet ourselves when we are feeling stressed. It's the first step in becoming more aware of what is going on in and around us.

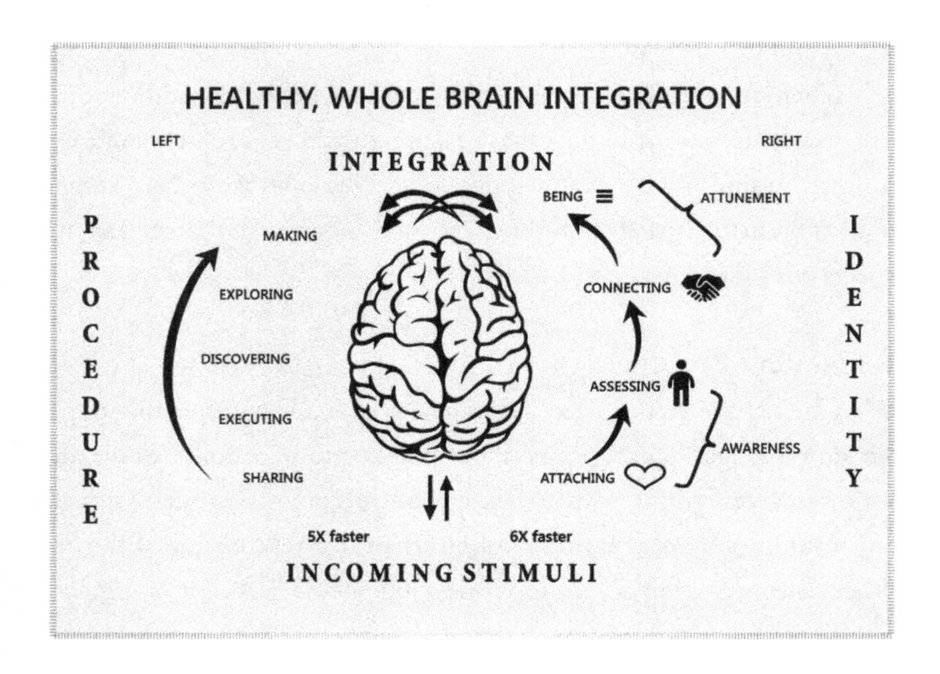

Counterclockwise and Counter Cultural

Let me repeat: our right brain reacts faster than our left. It "laps" our left, speeding to **assess** what's happening and searching to **connect** with God and others at six cycles per second. (The left brain, logical functions only run at five cycles per second.) That tells us something important.

No matter our bent—logical left or creative right—the brain processes information from bottom to top and right to left. That means when our central nervous system registers an impulse of energy or emotion, it checks in with our right brain to determine some things. First and subconsciously, our brain looks for answers that have the potential to provide calm or reassurance, create bonds, shape character, and form identity. Just as physically quieting ourselves, these hold additional keys to quieting us. On a very basic level, some questions the right brain needs answered include

- Am I safe, seen, soothed, secure? (**Attaching**)
- Is this situation good, bad, or scary? (**Assessing**)
- Am I alone? (**Attuning/Connecting**)
- Who is my example of how to behave in this situation? (**Individual identity**)
- Who are my people or where do I belong? (**Group identity**)[4]

Most likely we aren't even aware it's happening, but you and I "automatically" go on a search for the answers. These questions find their answers in our initial attachment provided by our primary caregiver.

Filtered through the lens of **attachment**, energy and information then move upward from here—adhering to our brain's counterclockwise flow (bottom to top, right to left). Information and stimulation always hit the right brain first. We learn to **assess** our surroundings, asking whether this is a good, bad, or scary person or situation. You may have heard of the fight/flight/freeze or fawn reactions? These originate deep within our brain in our amygdala and lymphatic system. If we remain in bad or scary much more than ninety seconds, we subject our system to more stress than it was intended to carry. Possible consequences include adrenal fatigue, cortisol overload, trauma, burnout, stress-related illness.

Together, considerations of attachment and assessment at a given moment create an overall **awareness** of what is going on and how we will proceed. This newfound awareness includes consciousness of feelings, sensations, and connections—our own as well as those of others. For whatever reason, if we feel alone or afraid, you and I will get stuck here. Moving forward requires the reassurance that we are not abandoned or alone.

Is there such a thing as a flourishing life without healthy self-awareness? Can we create our best work—the work that authentically resonates, influences, inspires, and connects us with others—if we ignore our experience? The answer to both questions is a resounding "no."

MAKER'S AFFIRMATION

Makers establish shalom —a balanced sense of peace and joyful anticipation —before taking creative action with left-brain formulas or processes.

I am a maker.

Maker Exercises

QUIETING

Supplies needed: crayons or colored markers

Coloring has been proven to release stress and anxiety, an increase activity in your brain's pleasure center. It is play, after all.

Before you begin, sit comfortably with your eyes closed and take a few deep, belly breaths. Put on some instrumental music and start coloring the design below. As you color, pay attention to maintain full breaths and a relaxed posture.

GRATITUDE

Have you wondered why weighted blankets garnered so much attention in recent years? Feelings of careful touch and being held harken back to attachment and can relieve anxiety. The gentle "squeeze" of deep pressure produces mood-boosting serotonin and sleep-inducing melatonin, as it reduces stress, causing cortisol.

Taking the time to "embody" our gratitude may be somewhat unfamiliar to many, but the benefits are rich. Experiencing gratitude in all its dimensions means we present our whole selves to God —to feel the emotional, mental, physical, and spiritual effects of what we appreciate. By doing so, we multiply the dynamics of being genuinely grateful, including increases in joy, spiritual awareness, self, organization, and self-control.

Adapted with permission from Adele Ahlberg Calhoun,
Praying the Psalms: Seeing God's Pattern in our Lives.
(Downer's Grove: InterVarsity Press, 2016), 21.

- What is a part of your body for which you are especially grateful? With eyes closed, picture its design, the sensations, and the functions it serves.
- Thank God for His genius. Thank your body for its hard work and care.
- Now, wrapping your arms around you, give yourself a genuine hug. As you do, take two cleansing breaths.
- Before you open your eyes, simultaneously stroke both arms from shoulder to forearm. Receive your expression of appreciation in your body.

REFLECTION

1. Do you consider yourself right or left-brain dominant? How does this express itself in your spiritual life?
2. When somebody asks you if you are creative, what is your response? Why?
3. Can you recall a time when someone wounded your creativity? What were the circumstances? How did it make you feel? Did you get past the injury or leave the practice behind?
4. Generally speaking, do you feel you have a healthy awareness of what your body, emotions, and thoughts are telling you? Which of these areas would it benefit you to pay more attention to?

MAKER'S PROMPT

Make something that represents something in creation that elicits awe or wonder. What makes you curious or gives you goosebumps?

Visio Divina

FOR CHAPTER 5

Christa Macfarlane, *Seeing Beyond* (2022),
acrylic on wood panel, Denver, Colorado.

It is the glory of God to conceal a matter,
But the glory of kings is to search out a matter.
PROVERBS 25:2 (NASB)

READ.

Read Proverbs 25:2. What do you think the author is trying to say?

REFLECT.

Read the verse again, highlighting anything that you observe.

- What does this say to you as you read today? Listen to what the Lord may want to tell you about it.

REIMAGINE.

Take a close look at Christa's MacFarlane's painting, "Seeing Beyond."

Sometimes all it takes to experience God's presence is a good look around. There are layers of dimension to who He is, all around us. Cultivating a habit of looking for things like the Lord's beauty, goodness, joy, or wisdom swings the door for His revelation open wide. We simply slow down, pay attention, and let ourselves be led. God hides in plain sight. Keep this in mind as you ask the Lord to guide you in this exercise. Relax and consider the elements that make up the painting.

- Describe the image. At first glance, what do you see?
- Do you perceive images hiding in this composition? Explain what surfaces.
- What part of God's beauty, goodness, joy, or wisdom is He revealing in the context of this Scripture and the painting?
- What does the painting enlighten about the words of Proverbs 25:2?

RESPOND.

How may a habit of seeing differently inspire you toward loving God, your neighbor, and yourself? Ask the Lord for His insight and capacity to help you pay attention for His opportunities to love.

CHAPTER 5

THE CALL TO ATTENTION

"The joyful presence of God is not somewhere else.
God is here, and so joy is right here, too."
– GEM AND ALAN FADLING, *WHAT DOES YOUR SOUL LOVE*

Floating around out there is a parable about two little fish who are swimming along one day. They meet up with an older fish who nods and says, "Morning boys! How's the water?"

Swimming on a bit further, one of the boys turns to the other and asks, "What's water?"

Sometimes we miss the most obvious things. Like the air (or water) we breathe, the environment we are in, or what influences us. Attachments are like that.

Our attachments swim in the deep waters of all our relationships and experiences.

There is a saying: "What goes down in the well comes up in the bucket." The base of our brain pulls data from one of two emotional wells: joy or fear. Thinking about ourselves as fish in a well, do we know which we are swimming in?

When healthy and secure, our attachment is founded on trustworthy, predictable connection and strong emotional bonds—this water is clear, refreshing, and sweet. If what flows in the well of our being is based on joy, all is (literally) well. Purified in relationship with our earliest caregivers, you and I can expect to enjoy a sense of security our whole life long.

If, however, our attachment source is poisoned by fear, its bitterness may sour our stomach and taint our days. In fact, since more than 60 percent of people struggle with attachment issues, it means some form of fear lurks in the depths of our wells. That fear manifests in what we make of life and in it. And, what we make matters to God.

Could it be possible that we don't pay attention to the water because it's all we have ever known? As makers, you and I need to discern our water source.

Wake Up!

Too many of us fumble through life half asleep. Numb. A lot of the time, we don't even notice. You and I have got to shake things up if we want our hearts, minds, and bodies to awaken. A general lack of awareness has us zombie-walking through our spiritual lives as if our bodies are separate from our souls.

But they are far from disconnected. In fact, God creatively speaks through our souls to inform our senses, and our senses to inform our souls.

Every morning when your feet hit the floor, pay attention!

Eyes and ears wide open, we discover newness of each day—filled with new pools of life experience. Will we dive-in to swim in those deep waters of joy or fear? (Guess what I hope you'll say?) Mindful of joy, every sunrise is mercy—a new opportunity to boldly and creatively reattach to the way we are meant to be. Becoming conscious and alert to what God is doing and inviting us to do by His side opens endless possibilities of purpose. Recapturing that awareness is living awake. Take notice!

Several years ago, some friends and I collaborated on a retreat we named "Awake." (Perhaps we should have called it "*Aware*" to be more accurate, but what's one letter? Back then, we didn't know what we didn't know.)

The idea began early one morning on the shore of a mountain lake. With sun on my back and coffee in hand, and with the Never Summer Range highlighted in the distance across the water, I asked a simple question of the Lord: "God, how do I combine how I creatively know and experience You with all that I've learned in the spiritual formation arena in a way that is shareable with others?"

You can probably tell that while my creative spiritual practices and classic spiritual disciplines may have run parallel in my spiritual journey, the bridge was out between them in my own soul. At that point, there was a clear disconnect. I listened for His answer.

As if He'd been on the edge of His heavenly throne waiting for me to ask, God answered pretty quickly with the outline for a retreat designed to experientially connect body, soul, and spirit with His Word. Clearly, this is what my soul had been searching for, and something that would certainly resonate with others. A few of my creative, spiritual powerhouse friends—Sue, Karen, Ellen, Nanci, and Mindy—jumped on board to share brainstorming, teaching, and creative touches for the once-in-a-lifetime getaway. Admittedly, the joy-filled time with our steering committee was one I took for granted. Putting the retreat together fed something deep in us all, I believe. God opened doors in ways we could not imagine as we planned a whole-life experience that included three days of teaching and creative encounters with Him.

The sold-out event drew women from all around the country to experience soulful elegance of God's best in the form of taste, touch, sight, smell, sound. Held in the beautiful Colorado outdoors, the three-day experience was wrapped tightly with Scripture and tied elegantly with the bow of His unique word for each woman. The spiritual atmosphere and beauty of our retreat brought heaven to earth.

Each day, we offered attendees new ways to awaken their life with God by engaging all their senses. The Word became flesh incarnated as we watched each woman connect—or reconnect—with the Spirit of God as well as with themselves. Incorporating Scripture, creativity, movement, and the five senses, sessions invited each woman to experientially take notice and respond to the Holy Spirit.

Soul Questions

Our goal throughout the retreat was to create opportunities for each heart, soul, and mind in the room to *fully* return to their First Love. With that in mind, we made a paraphrase of Deuteronomy 6:4 the theme of our retreat: "Hear O Israel, the Lord your God is One. . . You shall love the Lord your God with all your heart, all your soul, all your mind, and all your strength."

What I love about this verse is that it isn't philosophical or ethereal—it describes two powerful actions that God wants his people to take.

The first is to *hear*—and not as in "Listen up!" but to take action and respond obediently.

Did you know that Jews recite this commandment twice a day as part of their morning and evening services? Reciting this particular Scripture twice a day is an action that demonstrates its significance, and a beautiful response to what God is asking of them.

The second part of the verse instructs the reader to *love the One true God*. Like hearing and responding obediently, love is an action. With the children of Israel distracted by the worship of other gods of surrounding cultures, YHWH was calling his own to wake up and return to Him. What's more, He was asking them to hear and love with everything they've got. He was asking them to respond to Him full-heartedly, soulfully, mindfully, and with all their strength.

That's not the only place Jesus talks about love as an action. When asked what is the first and greatest commandment, Jesus cited Deuteronomy 6:4 then added, "The second is this: 'YOU SHALL LOVE YOUR NEIGHBOR AS YOURSELF'" (Mark 12:31 NASB). Like truly hearing and loving God, loving neighbor and self is not just an "emotion"—it requires a decision backed up by our actions.

But here's my point. Both Deuteronomy and Mark include the phrase "*with all* your heart and *with all* your soul and *with all* your mind and *with all* your strength." In addition to the importance placed on the Great Commandment, do you think these words would have been included in both the Old *and* New Testament if God didn't want us to be aware of these distinct parts of ourselves—and to be vigilant about caring for them?

There is something else powerful about these verses. The Word makes God's priority of connecting to Him, our neighbor, and ourselves clear.

Above all, the Lord crafted our original design for deep attachment with Him. So, notice for yourself:

- What does it mean for me to love God with all my heart, soul, mind?
- How am I doing at loving myself?
- How am I demonstrating an equivalent lovingkindness to my neighbor?
- What spiritually motivates my strengths and fuels my talents?
- Is that motivation swimming in the well of joy or fear?
- How does it change me and effect my purpose in God's world?
- Daily, there are a couple other important questions to ask the Lord to answer, too:
- How do You want to spend time with me today?

- How and what are You creating that I'm invited to "make" alongside You?

These are soul questions—intended for our soul more than for our *self.* You see, our self is a trickster. Without check, our self is egocentric and subject to errors of skewed self- perception, misguided motivations, and worldly influence. While our inner self informs some of the answers we are after, God created our soul as the eternal part of us—the container of our true identity as His beloved. Everlasting, discerning, and submitted to God's direction, our soul's answers are what lead us toward the daily uniqueness of our Great Commission—an artful one created for us by God himself. As we work our way through the book, I hope examining our hearts in this way becomes a regular and rooted habit.

Clarifying the answers begins with reconnecting with our desire for God and the beauty of life that surrounds us. Our hearts are built for this foundational, joy-centered attachment. This one true passion is reflected deep in our body and soul. Have you noticed?

Embodied

Our body, emotions, and mind are constantly telling us things—taking in information and using that information to help us interpret and respond to our world. Collaboratively, these parts of ourselves flow in an exchange of energy and information—within our minds, and between ourselves and others. In order to benefit from this dynamic process, we have to pay attention.

In his classic, *The Screwtape Letters,* C.S. Lewis tells the satirical tale of Screwtape, the top assistant to "Our Father Below" (Satan) and correspondent to Wormwood. Wormwood is a demon in training who is assigned to work the damnation of an ordinary young man as he keeps him far from the "Enemy" (God).

Summing up the lot of many today, Screwtape advises Wormwood: "Once he accepts the distraction as his present problem and lays that before the Enemy and makes it the main theme of his prayers and his endeavors, then, so far from doing good, you have done harm. Anything, even a sin, which has the total effect of moving him close up to the Enemy, makes against us in the long run."

Attachment issues, distraction factors, health problems, as well as the sheer pace of life today are just a few of the many things that can keep us distracted. Unfortunately, when we don't pay attention to our soul's deep needs, we will find ourselves plagued by inner unrest, loneliness, anxiety, and dissatisfaction. And when the world is crazy—think pandemic, politics, racial unrest, and Putin's war with Ukraine—it magnifies the problem. In fact, the American Psychological Association reported that between 2019–2021 rates of both anxiety and depression quadrupled in our country.

The good news: You and I can lower our unrest, loneliness, anxiety, and dissatisfaction if we stop ignoring our pain and longings, joys and fears. How? Glad you asked. Assessing how we are is an easy place to start:

Step 1. Sit still.

Step 2. Breathe deeply.

Step 3. Be in your body.

Step 4. Listen.

Whatever you do, resist the urge to blow through these steps too quickly. Take about 2-3 minutes to relax and consider each one. At every step, ask yourself this question: *What do I notice*?

Along with our body, emotions, and soul, the Lord often has something to say to our spirit or through His Word. Noticing makes listening to Him possible. Practice often.

Noticing versus Paying Attention

Noticing is where we start to assess things, but have you ever thought about the difference between noticing and paying attention?

In light of the zillions of bits of information that hit our central nervous system every day, attention allows us to go beyond noticing something. Dr. Amishi P. Jah, author and neuroscience researcher at the University of Miami, makes the difference between noticing and paying attention clear. On Brené Brown's *Dare to Lead* podcast, he said, "Attention selects and directs which subset of information we pay attention to. It controls our perceptions of things."

Along with what you and I notice, it's revealing to consider if there is something deeper God wants us to pay attention to. Where is our focus drawn? To stay connected with God and each another requires us to keep track of our attention.

I have lived on the eastern slope of the Colorado Rocky Mountains for most of my life—all but my birth to twelve Nebraska years. Back in middle school, the bus route I traveled to and from school looped past a beautiful panorama of the Front Range. Looking out the window for changes in the view—more snow, less snow, hazy or vibrant—I'd try to rally my bus-mates to marvel with me at the beauty most days. There were eyerolls and some teasing, but they knew I was right.

Part of a rare breed of Denver natives, my husband, Bill, has lived here his *entire* life. Guess who is more attentive to the mountains on a daily basis? ME. I can sketch them with my eyes closed. It's not that he doesn't notice them off in the distance. But he doesn't pay attention to the rolling climb of foothills, the shifting shadows, the daily shifts of atmospheric perspective, and the variety of hues jutting up to icy white peaks. He's just gotten *used to* the mountains always being there. Noticing versus paying attention. (Now, ask me who pays attention to the specific details of a golf course!)

Paying Attention Leads to Noticing Important Things

The simple steps outlined above can draw our attention to what is right or wrong in our life. But while noticing exposes things to our awareness, that is only part of the equation. Once we notice something, we make an often-subconscious split-second decision: will we act with intentionality and pay attention to what we've noticed—or just ignore it? There *is* a difference.

Noticing makes room for the closely related task of paying attention. Paying attention is an act of intentional engagement. By focusing our attention on something we have noticed or recognizing what is important right now, you and I take in that thing, task, or person more deeply. We stop and turn our gaze toward the object. And that to which we attend inspires curiosity or wonder in us and improves our engagement level.

But we don't *have to* take something we notice this extra distance. No one can make us.

For example, if you notice that it's hard to just sit and be, it may help to pay attention to what it feels like in your body, mind, or emotions. Or simply consider why it's hard to be still.

Finances pressing? Family demanding too much? Schedule overloaded? Priorities out of order?

Emotions out of whack? Body overextended? Friends let you down?

Does stopping like this make you anxious that you are "wasting time"? Does it elicit a deep sigh tinged with sadness? Or does a sense of happiness and peace accompany the experience?

Stop judging. Like waking up, you and I need to simply open our eyes. Without interpreting what we see as good or bad, simply observe what comes to the surface.

As professor and spiritual director Jan Johnson says, "Simply begin where you are."

When we are unaware—asleep at the easel of our lives—what you and I are called to make suffers. In contrast, when you and I take time to notice our internal landscape, we provide the Lord a canvas on which we can co-create.

At first, the idea of stopping to pay attention may sound tedious. But Socrates, a not-so-dumb philosopher, famously said, "An unexamined life is not worth living." For creatives, paying attention is the first step toward a more powerful and vibrant life—a life that lends authenticity and vulnerability to our work.

Paying Attention to Our Body

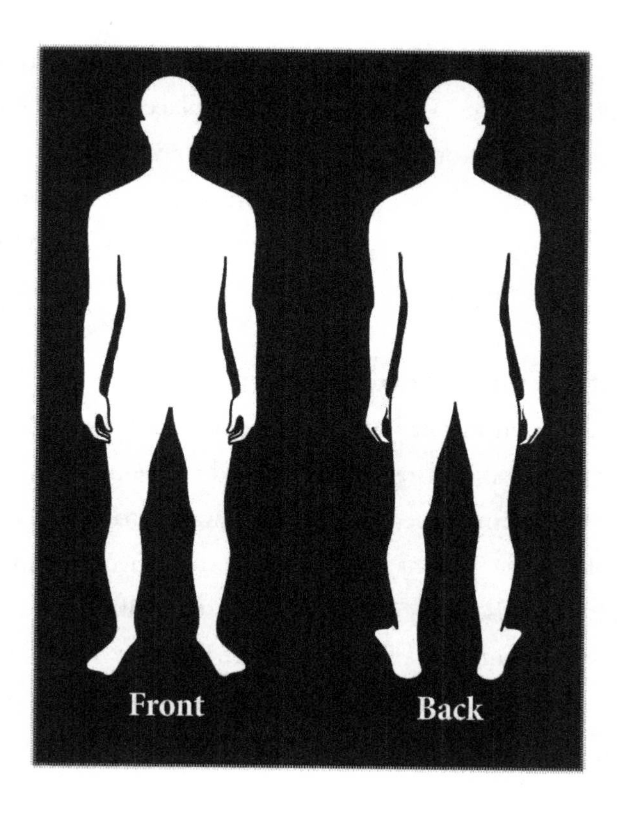

Look again at the flow of stimulus in your body and nervous system (bottom to top, right to left, remember?). Think about what it means to *be in* your body—fully aware of what it is experiencing. Now, noticing when your breath gets shallow, your pulse quickens, or you feel the heat of a blush should inspire you to pay attention, focus on your body, and ask: *What is my body trying to tell me right now?* Clenched teeth, tension in your neck, or anxiety in the pit of your stomach should make you ask the same question.

Could the answers be part of your spiritual journey?

Only if you *pay attention.*

It is smart to pay attention to what our bodies are trying to add to the conversation. In In *Renovation of the Heart,* Dallas Willard notes the body's importance in the ongoing process of our spiritual formation. He writes, "My body is the original and primary place of my dominion and my responsibility. It is only through it that I have a world in which to live. That is why it, and not other physical objects in my world, is part of who I am and is essential to my identity. My life experiences come to me through or in conjunction with my body."[5]

Paying Attention to Our Emotions

Just as we listen to our body, you and I must learn to listen to our emotions. I'm not suggesting that we be led by feeling alone but, upon reflection, our feelings reveal a lot. They matter to the heart of God, too. After all, the sensations and emotions that hit our central nervous system register in us before we consciously recognize them. According to Peter Scazzero, author of *Emotionally Healthy Discipleship*, "Christian spirituality, without an integration of emotional health, can be deadly—to yourself, your relationship with God, and the people around you."[6] He continues,

> When we deny our pain, losses, and feelings year after year, we become less and less human. We transform slowly into empty shells with smiley faces painted on them. Sad to say, that is the fruit of much of our discipleship in our churches. But when I began to allow myself to feel a wider range of emotions, including sadness, depression, fear, and anger, a revolution in my spirituality was unleashed. I soon realized that a failure to appreciate the biblical place of feelings within our larger Christian lives has done extensive damage, keeping free people in Christ in slavery.[7]

Our body and emotions have something to say. Some emotions are so intense, they can get in the way of us connecting with ourselves, God, and others. To review: neurologists have identified a group of seven basic emotions we share. Reading through the list, we will notice that only one—joy—is a positive emotion. The six remaining emotions are negative and commonly referred to as "the Big Six." Emotionally and physically, these can shut down our capacity to connect. They include fear, shame, sadness, disgust, anger, and hopeless despair.

These emotions are so intense, they show up in our bodies and our brains. Not only do they show up in our bodies through tension, headaches, inflammation, jitters, stomachaches—they also show up on fMRIs and SPECT scans showing us what part of our brain and internal organs is working—or not working well. Negative emotions literally short-circuit some processes of life, faith, and relationship like prayer, forgiveness, healing, love, joy, peace, patience, kindness, and self-control.

Sure, you and I can choose to buck up and blow past our body and emotions, but then we had better get used to frustration in our spiritual life. Our physical frame and feelings are a vital part of maturing—we have to learn to do and deal with hard things. I'd prefer a reset of awareness.

It's important that we learn how these seven emotions look and feel in us so that when they arise, we can be intentional about paying attention to their impact. Are they disconnecting us from ourselves? From God? Other people? Are they making us sick or depressed? Giving us migraines? Allowing us to gut out our overcommitments? Driving us to abuse alcohol, drugs, or food? Driving us into isolation? Causing us to withdraw from good and true people or things in our lives? Ignored, these negative emotions will impact anything we are in the process of making or doing.

Brushing them off with Pollyanna platitudes or steeled behaviors—even "faith-based" ones—will kill our best efforts toward knowing ourselves, beauty, or transformation. Paying attention helps us identify harmful patterns that are hurting us. Just watch.

Paying Attention to Our Mind

In addition to our body and emotions, Deuteronomy includes loving God with all our mind. Believe it or not, the definition of the *mind* as something distinctly different from the physiological organ of the *brain* only came about in the 1990s. (Crazy, I know.) It seems obvious that these things are different. But think about it: how would *you* define the mind?

Thankfully, smarter heads prevail (no offense).

Psychiatrist and pioneering interpersonal neurobiologist, Dr. Dan Siegel, explains that the **mind** (which resides in the brain) is the embodied and relational self-organizing process that regulates the flow of energy and information within ourselves and with other people, too. Read the previous sentence slowly and it will begin to make sense.

If you and I are not aware of the energy and information within our own minds and bodies, we cannot regulate either.

When you and I push left-brain-based arguments with religious clichés but without mindful awareness, we delude ourselves. Having no real idea what our body, emotions, and mind are going through places us at a disadvantage—you and I live life as physically, mentally, and emotionally dysregulated people. We "play with half a deck." Awareness of heart, soul, and *mind* is essential to our spiritual growth and maturity.

Mindfulness Angst?

Over the years, I've listened in on a lot of conversations between angsty Christians wary of spiritual deception. The term "mindfulness" really sets some people off. But I'm not talking about Buddhist or Hindu practices, or new age thinking. Awareness of what we sense and experience in our minds—that is, energetically and informationally—is none of those things. "Mindfulness occurs when we pay attention to our present moment experience with awareness and without emotional reactivity."[8]

Quite literally, to discard this important element of our personhood is narrow-minded—and quite the opposite of mind-full. God instructs us in Scripture to steward the energy and information within our body, mind, and spirit. There is no way to be fully aware and awake if we don't notice and pay attention to our senses, emotions, information, and energy of "*je ne sais quoi*" that our body processes.

You and I must also steward the energy and information that flows in our relationships with God and with one another. It is an important part of our whole-person, whole-brain discipleship. Once we understand that a large part of our creative call is about connecting through communication, the consequences of disconnecting from ourselves becomes clear: keen awareness of our body, emotions, and mind informs and energizes what we are able to receive and give. Every bit supplies what we make and how we make it.

God created human beings for this kind of connected awareness. Paul encouraged us regarding the importance of paying attention with a Spirit-based mindfulness when he wrote, "The person without the Spirit does not accept the things that come from the Spirit of God but considers them foolishness, and cannot understand them because they are discerned only through the Spirit. The person with the Spirit makes judgments about all things, but such a person is not subject to merely human judgments, for, 'Who has known the mind of the Lord so as to instruct him?' But we have the mind of Christ" (1 Corinthians 2:14–16 NIV).

As possessors of the mind of Christ, we obviously limit ourselves when we reject this key component of our emotional, relational, and spiritual growth. God encourages us to mature in wisdom and understanding (Hebrews 5:11–13).

The life-sucking things—including unhealthy attachment, broken relationships, and trauma—are heavy and wearisome. They deplete our energy and emotions, douse any spark of inspiration, and shut us down on all creative levels. Things that are life-giving to us fuel the energy of our unique creative fire.

What's the point? I hear you asking yourself. If we learn to notice when things tax, distract, or discomfort us—whether those things are internal or external—we can compassionately turn our attention to them rather than deny there is a problem. Rightly directed, paying attention can strengthen our connection with—and awareness of—God and the things He wants us to pay attention to that feel "off."

As those who love Jesus, we must get better at thinking about what we are thinking about, feeling our feelings, and knowing what our bodies are trying to tell us.

What Does "Quiet Time" Mean, Anyway?

Consider this: Many of us learned the importance of "having a quiet time with God," but few of us were taught that our quiet time should include a basic assessment of body and soul. *How am I, really?* is a solid, entry-level question with which to begin any time with God. Taking a minute to "get real" with ourselves—to notice and pay attention—both requires and generates awareness. That means a regular assessment of our whole self must be a mandatory practice. In all our beautiful ruin, paying attention enables you and me to bring ourselves honestly before God.

By learning to assess the state we are in, you and I elevate the priority of our time with God and the quality of ongoing life with Him.

Developing a sense of awareness of what is going on (inside as well as around us), you and I will get better at noticing when something is "off." That inner "rustling" signals a need for peace. It's as simple as paying attention. Honing practice of awareness begins in this straightforward way: you and I assess whether we feel peaceful—heart, soul, mind, and strength—or we don't. If we do feel peace, might I suggest taking a minute to bask in its goodness? However, if we don't feel that way, it is a cue to return our attention to God and start asking questions.

Connecting with our breath, body, and heart must become a regular creative practice regardless of our purpose in life, and especially if our purpose is to make disciples—and be a disciple—of Christ as He directed in Matthew 28. The psalmist grasped the significance and the simplicity: "LORD, my heart is not proud, nor my eyes arrogant; nor do I involve myself in great matters, or in things too difficult for me. I have certainly soothed and quieted my soul; like a weaned child resting against his mother, my soul within me is like a weaned child" (Psalm 131:1–2 NASB). When you boil it all down, God calls us to drop our pride and religious pretense, lose our power and influence, and opt instead to be quiet and rest in Him. Let Him see you and soothe you in the safety of His arms.

Habits that develop our capacity to notice and pay attention quiet us—they are disciplines that help us become conscious of how we are affected by what's going on in and around us. For that to be possible, we all need to dedicate time to settle down—experience quiet and rest.

By becoming aware of our distracted, noisy souls, our need to seek peace and the means to find it becomes obvious. Perhaps less obvious are the *good* things we must also rest from; even after joyful positive experiences, our central nervous system needs downtime. No matter what our age, unhurried times of soothing quiet help us recharge throughout each day—providing time to reconnect with ourselves and God.

Like those fish in the well water, you and I need to consider what our body, emotions, and mind are swimming in. It may be toxic to the life we want to be living with God, others, and ourselves. But, if you and I want to live vibrant, artful, and aware lives, what we notice and pay attention to is only part of the story. For that, we must pause long enough for the experience.

MAKER'S AFFIRMATION

Makers slow down in order to open themselves up to what God wants to focus attention on.

I am a maker.

Maker Exercises

QUIETING

According to scientists, nature walks can impart positive emotions, refocus your attention, lower stress levels, and instill purpose—all good, right-hemispherically dominant results.[9] Research shows optimal results with just two hours per week.

Get outside for a walk by yourself, but before you do, read through the instructions below:

- As you begin, take a few deep breaths to clear your mind and help you relax.
- Spend one minute noticing your footsteps—how the stride feels in your body, if you're light or tense, where the pressure strikes in your foot. Are you walking fast or slow? Is it easy or hard? Do your steps reflect your mood?
- Notice any distractions that occur. *Don't judge them.* Just notice each footstep and leave it behind as you keep walking.
- Turn your attention back to your steps.

After two minutes of noticing your steps, ask the Holy Spirit to draw your attention to anything noble, true, beautiful, or good that He'd like you to *pay attention to* during the rest of your walk. When something comes to your attention, don't rush—stop to take it in. Snap a photo with your phone, if possible. Study and reflect. Feel the effect in your body and emotions. (If you can't find the right feeling words review the Feeling Word list in the Appendix when you get home.)

- When you complete your walk, review the time. Overall, how do you feel emotionally and physically?
- Did the walk make you feel close to God? Distant from Him? Why?
- Journal about your insights.

GRATITUDE

Think of two or three things you are grateful for specific to this season of your life. Pay attention to each in detail. Why are they so special? What do these bring that is unlike any other time of your life? How does this feel in your body and emotions? What response does it evoke in you? Journal your responses.

REFLECTION

1. What does it mean for me to love God with all my heart, soul, and mind? Am I loving myself well? How am I demonstrating equivalent lovingkindness to my neighbor?
2. Am I looking at life—and those I encounter each day—dimensionally, or am I stuck viewing the surface?
3. What is the spiritual motivation behind my strengths and talents swimming in the well of joy or fear?
4. How does the source my motivation change me and affect my purpose in God's world?
5. In your own words, describe the difference between noticing and paying attention.
6. Circle which of the six negative emotions—fear, anger, shame, sadness, hopeless despair, disgust—do you struggle with most?

MAKER'S PROMPT

Abide with what is around you. Make something that highlights an element of nature that draws your heart into spacious dimensions with God. (Psalm 27:4)

Visio Divina

FOR CHAPTER 6

Gayla Irwin, *Stalking Bear* (2022), watercolor on paper, Denver, Colorado.

The Lord is my shepherd, I shall not want. He makes me lie down in green pastures;
He leads me beside quiet waters. He restores my soul; He guides me in the paths of righteousness for His name's sake. Even though I walk through the valley of the shadow of death, I fear no evil, for You are with me; Your rod and Your staff, they comfort me. You prepare a table before me in the presence of my enemies; You have anointed my head with oil; My cup overflows. Surely goodness and lovingkindness will follow me all the days of my life, And I will dwell in the house of the Lord forever.

PSALM 23 (NASB 1995)

READ.

Slowly read Psalm 23, picturing the scene in your mind's eye.

REFLECT.

Reread the Psalm, circling any words or phrases that quicken in you.

REIMAGINE.

Keeping the words of the psalmist in mind, reflect on the watercolor, consider the "bears" you've encountered—in the dark valleys, the wilderness, among your enemies, in your family circle, wherever.

- When and where has God's presence guarded and anointed your head?
- How is He demonstrating His presence and protection to you today? Make note of how you feel it in your body and emotions.

RESPOND.

With the eyes of your heart fixed on Him, thank Jesus for shepherding your life so far. Invite Him onto the path ahead of you.

CHAPTER 6

PRESENCE AND LIVING WITH BEARS

"I cannot imagine how religious persons can live satisfied without the practice of the presence of GOD. For my part I keep myself retired with Him in the depth of centre of my soul as much as I can; and while I am so with Him I fear nothing; but the least turning from Him is insupportable."

– BROTHER LAWRENCE,
THE PRACTICE OF THE PRESENCE OF GOD

The quietest, most peaceful place I know sits at the end of a dusty gravel road, down a packed pine path next to a lake on the west side of Rocky Mountain National Park. This lake has hosted generations of my family well—providing a legacy of laughs, generations of pinecone war-based friendship, scow racing celebrations, high mountain meadow hikes, and kitschy boat parades.

Eventually, as happens with extended and growing families, our collective clan outgrew the turn-of-the-twentieth-century family cabin. The need for more space took our branch of the family tree from the west side of the lake to its southeast shore where we leased another cabin for many years. I'd take our girls up for weeks on end while my husband held down his working world.

Basic but beautiful, mornings were still. There were no curtains in my room and the lake side of the house was a wall of windows so I would often awake early and stumble downstairs to watch the fog silently lift off the water's mirrory surface. Invariably around 7 a.m., a water-skier would break the mirror—cutting his path past us shortly before my bed-headed kids would wander in and the day would begin. After another day naming wildflowers on hikes and eating fruit snacks at the second meadow, I'd tuck my children into bed again, go downstairs, finish up dishes and read for a bit.

Our new post was at the lonely end of the lake where the road ends. Of the few neighbors, most were only at their cabins on weekends. Cell signals were sketchy at best and there was no chance of tuning a television antenna (there was no cable, and it was the pre-Wi-Fi era). Mostly, the peace and pace were wonderful, but some nights, the silence was deafening.

Occasionally, alone in the dark, I felt the haze of doom-laced dread and got a spooky feeling—like I was being watched. Especially on nights when the moon rise was late, I became viscerally aware that the old punch-lock doors and untempered, single-pane windows left the girls and me exceptionally vulnerable.

During the day, moose would often wade in the marsh near the inlet a few hundred feet down from our back door as deer hid nearby in the brush. At night, they would bed down. But not the bears. Dark is dinnertime. More than comfortable finding resident rubbish cans around the lake, these black bears knew right where to find the communal dumpster just before our road's dead end near where the moose like to wade.

I'll never forget one particular night when the bears must have been especially hungry.

They rambled their way in the dark, sniffing and snorting, climbing and tugging at the padlocks. BOOM! BOOM! BOOM-BOOM!

BOOM! They rocked the big steel container back and forth creating a sound like distant thunder.

I knew they'd never conquer the bear-proof bin, but I'd made bacon earlier that day.

We had chicken on the grill for dinner. My blood pressure ticked up, my body tense with fear. *How long before the bears pick up the scent and stalk down my driveway? Can they get in the door?* (They can open car doors, you know!) *Did I latch the window by the sink? Will they break the glass to get the food stores and trash here inside? As the lone adult responsible for our two small children upstairs, what was I thinking making bacon with bears in the woods?*

What if? Why didn't I? Where did I go wrong? Present panic. Past regret. Current self- doubt. . . and I was *ALL ALONE*!—with a bear outside. A very *real* situation, albeit imaginary outcomes. Later, after the sun came up the next day, it occurred to me how often the noise of fears—present and past—haunt my heart. Like a bear hunting bacon, my fears sniff out the smelly place of my soul and mind.

To paraphrase Genesis 2:18, it is not good for man (or woman) to be alone. There are bears out there, after all! So what imaginary bears come after you? It's only a matter of time before they come for us all, right?

The Third Component of Awareness

Since we've established that noticing and paying attention are only two of the three components of awareness, what is the third part we are missing?

The third aspect required for us to live with awareness is *presence*. Noticing and paying attention happen within us, as *individuals*. Presence builds on that ongoing engagement within, to create a posture of availability *beyond ourselves*. Acting on awareness, presence helps you and me experience life with God, ourselves, others, and the world around us more holistically. In a state of presence, you and I are "here and open" to one another as well as to our surroundings and circumstances. Presence lives free of agenda or judgment, full of compassion, and—most importantly—in the *now*. As such, it keeps the bears of past and future at bay.

Living in the present, you and I realize we are never alone. Between us, we exchange the life-giving energy of grace in the form of engaged relationship.

At the tip of the brain's right prefrontal cortex is the area that specializes in maintaining presence. This is where the liminal, neutral space of "now" lives. Like the semi-conscious space between sleep and wakefulness, it exists in the current *moment*—with no conscious thought of self, past, or future. In a present state, we are all in. Thanks to its function, you and I are able to pay attention to life scenarios more holistically before getting hung up or hyperfocusing on certain aspects of a person, project, or problem.

Under pressure, a person who has cultivated presence is relatively free of worry about the past or dread of the future. They aren't typically caught planning a grocery list during worship, zoning out in an important meeting, or outlining causes of an impending bear attack. When practicing presence, one can just "be." As a rule, people of presence live in—and take in—the present moment as undistracted, unhurried observers.

The best artists—as people who look first at the relationship of the whole *before* the sum of its parts—carry presence. In so doing, they see and notice nuances that others skip past.

For creatives, there is something about the whole of a being or scene that inspires us to look more closely at its parts. When you and I aren't present, we miss both. Want to be more creative? Invest in the practice of presence.

Wherever you and I go, there we are. Face it. Embrace it. To be a faithful presence in the world as Jesus calls us to be, we must do the work necessary to be physically, emotionally, spiritually, and mentally available in each moment. Whatever we are making in the moment, you and I have a responsibility to maintain presence with whomever and whatever we are making.

Too much time living in the past, distracted in the present, or ready to quickly move on to future plans and possibilities is a sure sign that we are living *absent*. Our being roams everyplace but where we actually are, which causes you and me to miss life's important stuff—like the delicious details of how sun feels on the skin after a long winter, how our friend's posture cries out for a hug, or how late day purplish shadows on a silvery, snaking river strike a stunning contrast to the straw yellows and raisin reds of the water willows nearby.

For me, one of my most precious memories as I was being "present" was seeing my dad's eyes dancing with tears of laughter. Apparently, the "famous last words" article I just read him struck his funny bone harder than I expected. Deep and infectious, his laughter spread throughout the family gathered around the table. Laughing at laughter. Together as a family.

Being absent not only makes us miss life's rich moments, it makes it hard to hear God—let alone ourselves, our partner, friends, or the old guy in the grocery store who just asked us for some help. Preoccupied, you and I are like cats chasing a flashlight beam on the floor—darting around, we miss what is real. Needless to say, we aren't at our best.

Presence and the Equilibrium of Shalom

Without building the capacity for the peace that quieting and rest provide, you and I can't sustainably live in the skin of presence. To our brain, peace is simply a low-energy state of joy. It exists in the same brain space as joy. (Cool, right?) *Shalom*, a balance of internal peace and joy, makes it possible to return to **presence** with God and others. Shalom is a state of presence. Presence is a state of shalom—the state of equilibrium that our brains are designed to live in.

When this gets out of balance, we literally sense it. That is why our level of shalom sets an especially useful benchmark for our bodies and souls (Matthew 28:16–20, 22:36–40). The oversupply of tension, pain, ruminating thoughts, increased heart rate, and the like may point out a drop in our capacity to be present. Awareness of such a dip sends us an invitation to change things—to catch our breath or catch up on rest. Once quieting to this becomes a habit, the shalom state of presence is something we consciously crave.

The alternative? In addition to the symptoms listed above, when we live without being present, you and I numb or ignore our need for quiet and rest. Instead, we do things like overload our schedule, park mindlessly in front of the TV, lose hours robotically gaming, or comfort ourselves with food or other substances.

Our heart, soul, and mind know what we need to thrive. Tuning out is not it. The capacity for rest and quiet is the balance needed for a rich and joyful life. Healthy creativity springs from the margin of what we establish for such.

So, do you and I sense the presence of shalom, or is *doing* overrunning our *being*? Is the noise of life muffling life's relational substance? Is hurry and hustle hassling our capacity to hear what matters? Do we even know? Caring for our soul with some honest answers encourages others to do the same.

Big Babies

From infancy, we seek soothing from overstimulation. Our brains need peace as well as joy. Gazing deep into pure baby eyes as I cuddle with our granddaughter, Thea, I notice when she averts her eyes and nuzzles into my shoulder. (I notice because *I want to keep gazing in her dove-pure eyes!*) But this is her signal to me: she needs to quiet before she can reengage with me. If I try to force her connection or play too soon, this little one will likely wriggle out of my arms and move onto something else. Much to her Ama's dismay, Thea withdraws and moves away. If I ignore her need for this, I am not being a faithful presence.

As adults, we are not so different. You and I are big babies. (I mean that in the best possible way.) We need times of high-energy connection (joy) balanced with low-energy quiet (peace). But honestly, do you and I recognize this need in ourselves and others? It's an important skill that few of us were intentionally taught to identify—let alone cultivate.

Many of us learn the social and emotional cues or body language that surround the need to quiet (like when we have locked eyes with a stranger for an inappropriate amount of time or violated a person's physical space by standing too close.) But a good number of us were never taught this. Some of us just push way past our need for quiet and rest, filling the space with more noise and activity. The Bible instructs, "The Lord is my shepherd, I will not be in need. He lets me lie down in green pastures; He leads me beside quiet waters. He restores my soul" (Psalm 23:1–3 NASB). Quieting with our Good Shepherd brings comfort and protection, establishes presence, reminds us who we are, and restores joy and peace to our soul. Shalom.

Toddlers

Have you ever been around an overtired toddler? Sometimes their exhaustion manifests in an overdrive of busyness; other times it shows itself in a full-on meltdown until Mama or Daddy scoop junior up and off to chill out with stories and bedtime.

Once in a while we need someone close to us like that who can better recognize when we need space and time to settle down. To maintain the ability to be truly present, you and I need to learn to value quiet and rest ourselves. Good news! This can be learned.

Recognizing the importance of this need makes it possible for us to experience and share God's peace. Believe me? According to UCLA Psychiatrist Alan Schore, the inability to quiet and rest is one of the largest risks of developing a mental illness or behavioral disorder—like anxiety, depression, addictions, or sleep problems.[10] In the context of their relationship, a healthy amount of shalom peace and joy is regularly shared—a comfortable current that strengthens, ebbs, and flows as a wave hitting the shore.

Healthy makers recognize the need for this kind of balance. Otherwise, what we create comes from a frenetic, unhealthy place in our soul. Our creative spark is generative—converting inspiration into the energy for our artform. Without the balance of quiet spaces, our souls will drain of the authentic capacity for creating. The integrity of our work is undermined.

A Good Return on Your Energy Investment

Some researchers claim that most of us only use 10 percent of our brain power, but attention experts argue that we use 100 percent of our brain all the time. That is, our brain is always working to determine what stimuli to process and what to ignore. That accounts for a lot of spent energy.

Oh, but what a return we get for that investment! When we aren't present, we might spend less energy, but what we *do* spend yields very little return.

So, how would you rather spend *your* energy?

As creators, how we spend our energy—and what we get in return—is important.

Learning how to be present to who or what God puts right in front of us is essential.

Just like other "habits," our capacity for presence alters our brain on a cellular level—grooving neuropathways of thought, emotion, and behavior—for better or for worse.

It's very difficult to maintain distracted behaviors once we learn to become absorbed in all the beauty, wonder, play, and grace that the present moment has to offer. But we will talk more about that later.

God with Us, *Now*

Let me underscore the importance: for Christian and non-Christian alike, mindfulness focuses on the present—it doesn't dwell in the past or project into the future. Christian mindfulness recognizes Christ with us—Immanuel—in *every* moment. Presence is an awareness and engagement with what is going on *right now*—with Jesus in the middle of it all.

A part of the brain, the insula, connects us with what's going on in our body in real time through sympathetic (fight-or-flight response) and parasympathetic (rest and digest) nervous systems. For example, our heart rate and blood pressure may shoot up when we are stressed about running late for an appointment (sympathetic). Laughing with a friend after the appointment is over allows our parasympathetic nervous system to take over—helping us relax, slow down, and conserve energy needed for heart health and digestion processes.

As mentioned, under stress our ability to be present shuts off, but there are things we can do to help us return to our senses. Maybe that is why Jesus told us to consider the lilies of the field and the birds of the air—living things that don't worry but are provided for by God. It's His way of encouraging us to focus on the present—in fact, He made this statement while preaching on a hillside, very likely gesturing to the birds and flowers visible at that very moment to his audience.

Enlisting tools to quiet ourselves turns on our parasympathetic system—helping return us to the present moment. Things we will practice at the end of the chapter like deep breathing, yawning, and Scripture meditation can enable you and me to quiet down so we can focus our awareness on what is right in front of us.

Energized and Fulfilled

Furthermore, those around us benefit. Presence—or the lack of it—creates a ripple effect, and other people are impacted. In fact, when we are present, it is like an offering of refreshing water to the thirsty, lonely, and distracted souls around us. In our presence, they get a taste of what practicing presence in their own life could offer them.

Painting a still life, working on a new business pitch with our team, writing a chapter, landscaping the yard, or collaborating with our partner to pick the right couch—whatever we are doing and whoever we are with—gets the benefit of our present awareness.

Make no mistake, however; this takes intentional effort on our part.

Cultivating presence increases our fulfillment. Author and speaker Jon Acuff explains,

"Being present is learning to be nostalgic about the moment you are still in."[11] You and I must savor experiences, feelings, and people—they are Godsent. With Him and them, be here *now.*

Like a good lyric stirs longing, a tender poem pierces the heart, a familiar aroma surfaces memories, or a beautiful tablescape invites us to gather, the aesthetics of our everyday experiences count for makers. Are we training to be present for what matters?

A shift to this way of life is fuel for the creative soul.

Showing Up Whole

The ability to remain in joy as we are present to experience people and things—take them in on sensory, emotional, mindful, and spiritual levels—cements understanding and knowledge. Here we are again working the knowledge-based *rumors* of life into the muscle of real life with God and others.

New neuropathways are formed as these connections strengthen within us. Along with them, new memories, relationships, discoveries, and truths emerge. Joy (the idea that we are delighted to be together) and peace (a deep, low-energy joy-state assuring us that all is well) depend on our capacity to rest.

In the flow of creative moments, presence allows us to show up wholeheartedly. In touch with all of who we are, distractions fade and the cream of our craft floats to the surface.

I don't know about you, but I appreciate dear ones with whom I can both laugh until it hurts or quietly sit and read. Sometimes, my brain and I just need rest. The opportunity to quiet and rest with others is hugely restoring—a recalibration for heart, soul, and mind.

God wanted rest for us enough to list it among the Ten Commandments. It is a command that He Himself observed after finishing his creative work in Genesis 1–2. He stopped and assessed what He made each day, ultimately labeling it "good." He knows that you and I need unhurried space to keep body, soul, and mind in check, yet we squander His provision for that need. In doing so, you and I forfeit growing in our capacity to be present to the Lord, ourselves, and one another.

Self-presence-less

In my family of origin, the word was *GO!* We pressed on and through hard things. Talking about negative emotions? None of that. Training for a sport—yes! But complaining about sore muscles? Don't be a hypochondriac. Having an off day because you're tired? Fine, just don't be "owly," as my dad used to say.

Familywise, I wouldn't say we were overly driven, just busy. And there was a highly held value that we were not to "impose on other people." "Good Christians" should never voice pain or weakness, right? The cumulative subtext taught me to ignore my body, emotions, and need for help—to the extent that at twenty-four, I was hospitalized with massive blood clots in my lungs after a week of ignoring headaches, body tension, and the ongoing work stress I was under.

I am a bucker-upper. Not wanting to complain, my solutional track record shows that I ignore things I shouldn't. I don't reach out when I should. Sometimes, I deny situations, feelings, and emotions that need to be acknowledged.

And this lack of awareness nearly killed me.

Objectively, when I live this way, I am not being compassionate to *myself*. And as a result, my availability to be present to God and others suffers. Relationships are diminished.

Creativity is crippled. As I've proven and lived to tell: there's no great virtue in self-ignorance.

Old habits die hard. Today, I still have to work at listening to my own body and soul. Remembering to check in with myself—to assess when quiet and self-care are in order or needs need to be expressed—is key. Presence to self isn't just for other people. If we know and esteem its value, we learned it from our experience with others. It is meant to be shared between us.

Spiritually, I find this to be especially true.

Sustainable Presence

One time, I was in the room when someone asked Dallas Willard what one word he would use to describe Jesus. You'll never guess what he said. After thinking for a moment, Dallas responded, "Relaxed." I never would have thought to apply that word there! To me, Dallas's description screams *presence* (in a nice, Christian tone, of course).

To be relaxed is to be peaceful and purposefully unhurried on all levels—free of tension (body) and anxiety (mind and spirit). Unrushed, unworried, and available to those He was with, our Messiah got an awful lot done each day, yet he remained relaxed—modeling presence as He lived each moment.

Jesus lived rhythms that sustained presence. His earthly life was peppered with spaces necessary for self-awareness. Wandering the dusty roads and towns of Israel, He was never in a hurry—never frazzled by ETAs or agendas. It freed Him to encounter people in the moment. On earth as it is in heaven, He moved at the speed of grace set by His Father, the needs of others, and His own healthy boundaries. With the clock ticking on his three short ministry years, Jesus consistently paced Himself by getting away to pray—to quiet, rest, and connect with God's heart for direction, comfort, and reassurance. Then, from a refreshed soul, He was able to play, laugh, and enjoy a good meal with friends. A relaxed manner, rooted in our ability to practice presence, creates an ideal environment for disciple-making.

If and when circumstances called for it, Jesus' relaxed nature could also allow Him to overturn marketplace tables or level a measured rebuke, sure that his actions flowed from an unweary, unharried, and connected soul. His presence is shalom.

When it comes to growing and maintaining presence, what practices and rhythms do you and I engage? What habits help us find quiet and rest our soul? Keep in mind, whatever our method, the goal is to draw our attention to God, self, and others, right now. Perhaps we enjoy traditional spiritual disciplines like silence and solitude. Or maybe what centers us is a less traditional endeavor such as going for a moseying walk with our heart, soul, and mind tuned in to what we are doing and who we are doing it with—God or another friend.

It might even be a game we play with God. Frank Laubach—a missionary, mystic and literacy "apostle" to Filipino Muslims within the Moro tribe—turned presence into what he called "The Game of Minutes." For at least one second every minute, he endeavored to turn his thoughts to God. Doing so kept Laubach in present and prayerful interaction with his Maker.

Similarly, lay Brother Lawrence practiced God's presence by praising Him over the pots and pans of his Christian kitchen life/work in a monastery.

Tethering to the Present

For disciples of Jesus, an awareness of God's constant and abiding presence is fundamental. Almost as important is an awareness of *our* presence to God.

If this sounds difficult, think again. It's just a habit, returning our attention to God anytime we notice that our attention, actions, or emotions have drifted. Anytime we become aware that our souls are untethered to the present—adrift in the past or future—all we have to do is stop, look for God's presence, and enjoy that He is with us *here and now.*

No matter what you and I are facing, three truths can tether us to God:

1. We are never alone because He is always with us in our daily endeavors (Matthew 1:23)

2. He has unending desire for connection,\ and finds unconditional delight in each of us no matter what we are up to (Zephaniah 3:17)
3. In Him, our souls are safely kept (2 Timothy 4:18)

Annie's Daily List

Let me tell you about Annie.

A PGA golf pro and a two-time cancer survivor, Annie is a noticer, a marveler, a twinkling light. Nearly every day she wears bright sea blue to match the color of her eyes and bangles engraved with inspirational sayings. She teaches at a couple golf clubs and coaches the state champion golf team at a private high school nearby.

Apparently, golf has taught her some life lessons. From what I've heard, breaking down a golf swing requires incredible amounts of presence—focus, as it were. Elements of stroke, power, weather, green conditions, spectators, and competitive foes must be considered for a golfer to make the perfect shot. Through years of practice, Annie learned how to break down and simplify each technical detail. She has mastered her own presence and focus and teaches her students to do the same.

Recently, to celebrate another friend's big birthday, I traveled with Annie and a bunch of women to the unsalty shores of Lake Michigan. I didn't know Annie well, but I knew that standing at this shoreline was on her proverbial bucket list. Over our five days together, we enjoyed beautiful early fall weather, a lot of hilarious laughter, and Annie's "treasure hunt" for the number seven. (Scripturally, it is a perfect number, you know?)

As we trod the beach, dodging waves and sharp shells while striving for 10,000 daily steps, I got to know her story. I learned that Annie was bent on accomplishing everything on that bucket list of hers, and that—

according to her doctors—her time may be short. The latest diagnosis (her third): stage 4 metastasized breast cancer had taken up residence in her bones and in the breathing-space of her lungs.

That gut punch would drop me, I suspect, but not Annie. She said each round has taught her how to let things go so she can be present to what really matters.

At sunset the day we arrived, seven was in the clouds and in the profile of an old red lighthouse. In the days that followed, all of us took up the hunt—seeing sevens in rocks, cookies, and latte foam; on trees, license plates, street signs, sailboat sails, and our baggage carousel. Her game made us notice, pay attention—to stand in the place we were living. As a group, we cheered one another on, delighting in the conquest of another number seven for Annie. The diversion made us creatively curious—we looked at things a whole new way. By taking our eyes off her diagnosis, Annie taught us joy! And, I'm fairly certain, it was God's gracious game to help her stay present. Without question, it made me more present, too. Our trip ended with prayer-bent hands and full hearts. We are with Annie all the way on the journey ahead of her. . . and she knows it.

It seems to me that most of us make being present way too hard on ourselves. Do we dwell in the past and worry about the future because we doubt His goodness or our own? Perhaps we think we harbor ourselves better than He does (*eyeroll*). As you and I strive to become more present to others, we will drop these doubts as we witness God's goodness and faithfulness.

Growing

Choosing to grow presence and connection as a way of life, you and I avoid detachment and distraction by things that will never bring us the joy and peace we desire.

Life is full of stressful, hard, and fearful things—those of both the daily and catastrophic variety. If you and I are honest, we know in our bones that we have an urgent need to grow our capacity to quiet and rest.

Where we put our focus matters. Learning to pay attention to the places our mind, body, and soul drifts helps us reverse the tide of life and stay present in the moment. When you or I ignore the physical, emotional, and relational aspects of life—or deal with them as an afterthought—we do ourselves a disservice. Guided by the Holy Spirit, maintaining purposeful presence enables us to wring out all the joy, peace, compassion, and comfort God has for us. In quiet and calm, our spacious souls stretch out—giving and receiving care and attention required for a robust life.

Annie's quest for the number seven testifies of God's goodness and demonstrates peace in her present circumstance—helping maintain her focus throughout each day. Quieting her spirit like this keeps Annie in the present and ushers in *shalom.* By definition, God is with her and blessing her. Her "game" hones presence, helping her to experience little "winks" of God's love and blessing. It quiets her throughout the day and provides hopeful expectations of the future, bringing her endless delight.

Quieting in a Noisy Church?

Without presence there is no quiet for our souls. As a spiritual practice, quieting trains our character to be like Jesus. During Jesus' days on earth, He was very aware of the needs and motives of His heart, soul, and mind at all times. He loved God, His neighbor, Himself—even his enemies—and He was able to stay aware of their needs and motivations. When He was with others, He was *with them.*

He seamlessly wove presence into an aware, responsive, relational life. Within His humanity, Jesus left room for interaction with His

Father and the miraculous action of the Holy Spirit. So why is it that practices that help us quiet—those that help build awareness of what is going on in our heart, soul, and mind—are not typically accommodated or encouraged in most faith communities?

Oh sure, once a year (or ten years) when we go to a church retreat, we might be encouraged to spend time doing some of this stuff. But in most churches and small groups, the weekly order of service understandably doesn't afford a lot of time for the quiet and rest our souls need to become present. What is wrong with a brief pause to allow our souls to catch their breath? Or a reflection question followed by a few minutes to, well, reflect? In the midst of our busy lives, doesn't it make sense that our leaders help us carve out space for presence?

At all points of becoming like Jesus—in presence and otherwise—there are two questions we must ask ourselves:

1. How does my life reflect what is going on in my heart, soul, and mind right now?
2. How is God encouraging my *relational* spiritual growth with Him and others? In other words: Where do I need to show up in this moment? How can I invite others to do the same?

Developing our capacity to quiet and connect is how we fight the noise and distractions that would keep us from presence. As an essential right-brain, relational skill, presence helps us move toward our double-faceted goal to *be disciples of Jesus* and *bring others along in their discipleship.* Living life this way, you and I shine light in the dark for one another. So the next time the bears seem to be lurking outside our door, the light of quiet presence can help us remember that we are not alone.

MAKER'S AFFIRMATION

Makers reject a life of dark despair. Instead, they relax in the light of God's love, care, and community.

I am a maker.

Maker Exercises

QUIETING

Breath and the written word.

When we are calm, we are present. Presence enables us to learn, understand, relate, and take in more. Centered on Christ, such mindfulness encourages authentic integration of our whole being—spirit included. The right hemisphere is dominant in the formation of character and values. To fully enter in as disciples of Jesus, we must cross this threshold of acceptance—the light and warmth of which beckons us.

- Start by lighting a candle to remind you of the light and warmth of His presence. He is with you. As the smoke of the match and wick ignite, watch it rise heavenward. Enjoy the flame's dance and the sense of God's invitation to be right where you are with Him.
- Next, close your eyes and breathe deeply from your belly for two minutes (or until you feel at ease).
- Then, continue to breathe deeply as you listen to the lyrics of "He Will Keep You/Psalm 121" by Sovereign Grace.
- To finish, inhale a couple more times deeply through your nose. When you think your lungs are as full as they can be, sip in one more bit of air through your mouth. Then release a sigh as you exhale through your mouth. Continue to reflect on what you've just heard.

GRATITUDE

Who helps you feel brave when you are afraid or under stress? How does their presence remind you of God's? Picture their presence. Feel it in your bones, the sinews that connect them. Breathe deep and picture the last time you felt their companionship. Cherish the memory by recalling the details. Thank the Lord for the model their care provides for you. Journal your thanks in your Gratitude List.

REFLECTION

1. What imaginary bears come after you?
2. What practices and rhythms do you engage in regarding growing and maintaining presence? What habits help you find quiet and rest for your soul?
3. How does your life reflect what is happening in your heart, soul, and mind right now?
4. How is God encouraging your *relational*, spiritual growth with Him and others? In other words: Where do you need to show up in this moment or season?

MAKER'S PROMPT

Make something that reminds you of where you are. Then, keep your creation somewhere you'll see it often to remind you to be fully "there."

Visio Divina

FOR CHAPTER 7

Jennifer S. Freeman, *Foggy Day* (2021), oil on canvas,
Santa Barbara, California.

The Lord your God is in your midst,
A victorious warrior.
He will exult over you with joy,
He will be quiet in His love,

He will rejoice over you with shouts of joy.
ZEPHANIAH 3:17 (NASB 1995)

READ.

Read Zephaniah 3:17 slowly, pausing between each line to *picture* what is being said.

REFLECT.

Read the verse a second time, circling what stands out.

REIMAGINE.

Upon a third reading, think about which line do you need to hear most today. Rest in those words for a minute. Don't rush. Feel how the Lord is showing up for you in this moment.

Some days, it feels like my creativity flows more easily than others. Conditions can't and won't always be perfect. Those days, making is a struggle at best or a brawl when my fears really start flying. On occasions when it seems easier to walk away from the easel or the assignment, there are important creative decisions to be made. Fight? Flight? Freeze? Or . . .?

Jenny Freeman explains her oil painting, *Foggy Days*, as a reminder that when she can't decipher the horizon line, it is an opportunity to live by trust. Often if we stay connected with God beneath marine layers of our fear, we will find Him fighting, exulting, quieting, and rejoicing over us. In this peace, we cut through the mist able to create with Him again.

- How does *Foggy Days* feel to you?
- What does it surface in your heart, mind, and body?

- In terms of your encounters with creative resistance, what is the invitation Zephaniah and the painting extend? (Think about your work, making, relationships, stresses—any category God surfaces.)

RESPOND.

Prayerfully respond to the words you receive. Thank Holy Spirit for what He shared with your heart.

CHAPTER 7

BATTLING CREATIVE RESISTANCE

I have a problem. It goes like this:

Sometimes I think to myself that nothing I'm writing in this book hasn't already been written, said, or at least thought about by most people. After all, in the fifteen years that I have been gathering my thoughts—along with the neuroscience data to support it—it seems like a whole bunch of other people with much bigger platforms have gained followings on the topic. MY topic. I think to myself, *If I would have written this book earlier, maybe it would have mattered, but why bother now?*

Sometimes I entertain the idea that the timing of this book is God's way of keeping me in the humble lane. After all, I tell myself, it would be silly for me to think I can add anything to the conversation. I mean, who do I think I am?

See? Consciously and unconsciously this mental banter holds a gun to my creative head. This self-talk bangs wild warning shots every time I encounter something creatively challenging and find myself projecting failure, regretting something I didn't do, or condemning my audacity to try as posing and pretense unbefitting a Christian. Bullets whiz by my past, zing at the future, and lodge themselves—at least for a time—in my current sense of identity.

Who knows? Maybe you have similar thoughts sometimes. Maybe your thoughts are fueled by the belief that you're just not creative or the malaise of procrastination. Whatever the case, we try to rationalize our creative resistance away instead of pausing to experience the feelings and reflect on why we are resisting our creativity to begin with.

Remember what we've learned about the way our brain works and read that last sentence again. Neurologically, psychologically, physiologically, and emotionally, rationalizing (a function of the left, linear side of our brain) occurs *after* we experience the right-brain effects of creative resistance. Our rational mind trails behind.

When you or I notice that stuck, resistant feeling creep over us, it is time to consider what negative emotion is keeping us from thriving in the present by assaulting our mind with past failures, future anxieties, or our current wounded identity.

Creative resistance is a real thing. Many would define it as a force that opposes our noble creative efforts. It is much more than a momentary lack of focus or deficit of ideas. And the reality is, most of what we've been told about creative resistance is a myth.

Creative Resistance Is, at Its Root, Fear

Though it may wear the socially acceptable disguise of "creative resistance," at its core, fear lurks within. So, let's call it what it is. Creative resistance freezes the artistic juices in our veins.

Fear is a creativity cutthroat, a relationship killer, a joy assassin. Entering into any creative task with a sense of it stalking us will surely keep us in chains. In its more elusive forms, fear may slither into your life as subtle avoidance, shame, dread, drifting despair, procrastination, or emotional numbness. Unaddressed, it can grow into a big hairy monster that roars with rage, disgust, terror, judgmentalism, addiction, condemnation, comparison, or narcissism. Sometimes more than one.

To normalize creative resistance as a necessary evil only fuels the crackling fire of anxieties and ultimately encourages the forfeiture of our best creative work. Sure, sometimes when you and I need to put on our creative thinking caps, resistance can come out of the woodwork.

But that doesn't mean we just accept it.

In his creative classic, *The War of Art: Break Through the Blocks and Win Your Inner Creative Battles*, author Stephen Pressfield asserts, "Resistance by definition is self-sabotage."

I believe that fighting creative resistance is a kingdom-worthy battle. The enemy of our souls loves the opportunity to leverage our fears (and some of his own) against us. I mean, what better way to limit our imaginations and aspirations for the kingdom, right? He loves when we set up our own paralyzing paper tigers. Growling in our heads, they bring our fears and his lies to life.

For years, such snarling kept me out of art classes and convinced me to devalue or give away my paintings. I offered my makings to good causes and never considered signing anything I'd made. Know why? The reasons were twofold: 1) I had bought into the lie that my work only mattered if it was "traditional ministry," and 2) I rationalized that I would start signing things someday once I'd mastered whatever technique was featured.

Repeat after me: *I will no longer tolerate creative resistance to stall the good work God has for me.*

Up until now, if you and I have bought into the idea that creative resistance is a merit badge of creative honor, we need to tear it from our uniform. Now. Creative resistance is not a trophy of accomplishment but a sign of opposition to who and what God made us to make with Him in this life.

The idea that you and I just have to learn to live with it is untrue.

Regarding fear and creative resistance, Pressfield explains, "Fear doesn't go away. The warrior and the artist live by the same code of necessity, which dictates that the battle must be fought anew every day."[12]

What Pressfield is getting at is that creative resistance is a real thing—but you and I don't have to let it rule over or intimidate us. If we do, we automatically become the underdog in the fight.

So, turn on the light, look under the bed if you must, do whatever you must to root out the besetting fear that holds you hostage and limits your life's art. Daily. In order to offset fear-based resistance and live a creative life, there is no other way. Begin by paying attention to the tracks that lead to the places where creative resistance stalks you. Most likely, there is a well-worn path.

Or two.

Here are some wise reflection questions for our next battle:

- What behaviors do I recognize as telltale signs that I'm stuck?
- Is there a pattern of when it surfaces in my work, relationships, or schedule?
- Where do I feel creative resistance in my body?
- How does it feel—physically, mentally, or emotionally?
- What offers relief and allows me to return to creating again?

The fear that fuels our creative resistance can be subtle—like a buzzing fly—or really intense—like condemnation of our very existence. Either can be used by Satan against us, and is something we have to war against

Tolerating the shrill internal alarm of fear in our body makes it difficult—if not impossible—to create anything of value. It is counterproductive to our creativity. This is war, people! Healthy fear of mountain lions, stepping out in traffic, and lecturing naked is *not* what we are talking about. The kind of fear I am addressing keeps us from starting, stops us mid-mission, or wires a spectacular-but-destructive explosion at the end of our artful project.

Each of us has adopted behaviors to take the sting out of life. In his book *Becoming a Face of Grace,* author Ed Khouri writes about what he has labeled the "4 Deadly Ps." He explains how Perfection, Performance, Pleasure-seeking, or Pain-avoidance infiltrate too many religious circles and lives.[13] These unconscious motivations occur when you and I attempt to live our lives simultaneously attached to God and fear. If we let them, they will warp who we become.

Fear fortifies its amygdala-based bunkers with ideas of creative resistance. If we try to take this hill alone, we will die on it.

Post a lookout in your soul! We don't have to allow this fear-driven creative resistance to occupy our central nervous system or claim territory in our lives. And even if we expose and banish creative resistance, it will try to creep back in. So, we must stay diligent.

In addition to our own wrong thinking, the enemy of our soul knows how to bait us to the hillcrest—encouraging us to keep fear hidden, mask our weak spots, fake ability, or feign courage.

Unrelenting, he strives to steal our hope, strap our resources, and sap our strength.

Fighting him with the false sense of superior firepower provided by left-brain strategies, we will lose the battle. Satan knows if he can keep us feeling alone and afraid in the daily skirmish, we are walking right into his trap. So, don't go it alone.

When you and I feel uninspired to create, odds are high that we are *not* feeling joyful. It is a sign that we are operating out of some form of fear—and fear is a shapeshifter. It may come to us as feelings of incompetence. It could be falsely disguised as humility, or approach bellowing with bravado to divert attention from the problem at hand. These are just stall tactics.

The myth becomes reality when we use it to buy time or excuse our lack of progress. In such cases, as romantic as it may sound and despite all its posturing, creative resistance is a flimsy excuse for not getting our work done.

Refusing to confront creative resistance takes prisoner our relationships with God and others. But it is zero hour. Consider our enemy, and the significant kingdom cost of surrendering our creativity to him.

For some, the ferocity of the firefight may be greater than for others. Nonetheless, surrender is not an option.

Fear and Trauma

As mentioned in a previous chapter, fear is an umbrella term for the other six neurologically recognized, God-given emotions that you and I experience (others include anger, sadness, shame, disgust, and hopeless despair).

To be clear, everyone needs *healthy* fear in order to remain safe and well. But, healthy or not, fear influences us greatly as cortisol and adrenaline seep into our system. Deep in our brain—the amygdala, to be exact—we receive an alert. We fight, take flight, freeze, or fawn.

Healthy fear is a good thing. Sometimes, we need to feel the goading of fear. This response helps us navigate immediate responses to danger. The amygdala is designed to sustain fear-based reactions for about ninety seconds (just enough time to push back from peril or outrun the next slowest prey).

Whether incited by something horrific or the mundane disregard of our basic needs, remaining in this heightened state of fear any longer than that creates trauma within our bodies.

How do we know if we are living in fear? If we are living with a constant and false awareness that we need to earn or do something to avoid negative outcomes, we are likely operating in a state of fear. This state negatively affects our body, soul, and relationships—not to mention our art. Abandoning our lives to toxic, fear-based trauma, we lose the battle. Our creative freedom is limited.

Respected trauma research author, Bessel van der Kolk, MD, has spent his entire career studying the causes and effects of trauma on adults and children. Incorporating the latest neuroscience and attachment theory, he interprets emerging research so people like us can understand its implications, as well as effective modes of trauma treatment. He writes, "We have learned that trauma is not just an event that took place sometime in the past; it is also the imprint left by that experience on mind, brain, and body. This imprint has ongoing consequences for how the human organism manages to survive in the present. Trauma results in a fundamental reorganization of the way mind and brain manage perceptions. It changes not only how we think and what we think about, but also our very capacity to think."[14]

For those who find themselves in a constant skirmish with trauma from unhealthy fear, lay down your weapons. Or if you, like so many, think there are more substantive, spiritual things that Christians should deal with, Jesus says it's time to make peace with your creativity. The fear behind your creative resistance has no ammunition against our faith-based coalition. Rest assured, "the battle belongs to the Lord" isn't just good Old Testament material. No well-meaning doubter, jeering wannabe, or high wall of hell can stand against God's creative call on our life. So next time creative resistance imprisons us, we must use everything in our souls to break out.

In art school, I learned a foundational principle of color theory: the darkest light is always lighter than the lightest dark. This is true in the dark spiritual battles we face every day, so take heart! The Bible encourages us, "You are the light of the world. A city that is set on a hill cannot be hidden. Nor do they light a lamp and put it under a basket, but on a lampstand, and it gives light to all *who are* in the house. Let your light so shine before men, that they may see your good works and glorify your Father in heaven" (Matthew 5:14–16 NKJV).

As weak, traumatized, and oppressed as we may feel under the weight of our creative resistance, we bring light to the world and glory to God in our creative ways. Even if our light seems dim to us, the darkness cannot overpower the light we carry.

Know Your *Real* Enemy

Before moving on, it's important to point out one last thing. There is a big difference between a creative *block* and creative *resistance*. Too often these terms are used interchangeably but they are far from the same thing. As part of my own creative practice, I make an important distinction between the two.

When any of us experience a creative block, it is about lack. Unlike creative resistance, creative block is not about unhealthy fear or a spiritual attack. The effects of a creative block tell us that the lack of something we need is hindering our creative action. Examples may include a lack of:

- Sleep
- Nutrition
- Life balance
- Time
- Exercise

- Technical skill
- Health
- Finances
- Mindset, or
- Coffee (this is truer for some of us than others)

With tactical honesty, a shot of strategy, and a few well-placed campaigns of self-discipline, we can learn how to defeat these obstacles and get on with our creating. In most cases, the skills we need to defeat creative block include some form of self-awareness and self-care.

On the other hand, creative *resistance* is rooted in unhealthy fear. Get the difference?

Know your enemy and act accordingly.

Where Do We Go from Here?

Escaping the bondage of fear and reactivity in order to experience restoration requires reclaiming lost territories of joy in our life. The spaces where we experience joy by reflecting and connecting is where our creative nature takes its first breaths of freedom. Like oxygen in our lungs, God designed delight as an essential part of our makeup—made manifest in our sanctified, set-apart, and shining heart, soul, and mind (1 Peter 1:15–16). Creative freedom in Christ lights us up! In cities and individual homes, our joy shines as a bright light for others.

To defend ourselves in the daily fight against creative resistance, the first counterattack is to get back to our quieted selves—the state of heart, mind, and spirit explored in chapter six.

In upcoming chapters, we will explore more specific ways to find our joy again and launch a blitzkrieg that will bring freedom to us and others on the creative discipleship road.

MAKER'S AFFIRMATION

Makers process fearful emotions with God and others on the spiritual journey. Recognizing and sharing creative struggles reminds them that they are never alone.

I am a maker.

Maker Exercises

QUIETING

Close your eyes and think about one good decision you made today. For instance, maybe you like what you decided to wear, what you ate for breakfast, or how you made time to meet your friend for coffee. Then,

- Reflect on the specifics of what made that decision good to you.
- As a result, how do you feel now—emotionally, physically, and mentally?
- Set a timer for two minutes, close your eyes, and breathe deeply as you revisit all those feelings.
- Thank God and then celebrate yourself: you make good decisions!

GRATITUDE

Did you know that shalom isn't just about peace? It is the wholeness that results when joy (the high-energy delight in being together) perfectly balances peace (a low-energy form of joy that manifests in calm). In Israel, shalom is a greeting that seals when people come in and go out—covering their lives.

Recall a time you felt deeply at peace recently. What were you doing? Was anyone else part of your experience? With all your senses and emotions, revisit what it was like in detail. Add this to your Gratitude List. Then, share with God (and anyone else involved) how thankful you are for the gift of peace left in your soul.

REFLECTION:

1. Understanding that creative resistance is simply fear, what forms do you commonly encounter? (Check any that apply)
    - Comparison
    - Self-doubt
    - Impostor syndrome
    - Perfectionism
    - Procrastination
    - Lack of motivation
    - Drivenness and pressure to achieve external rewards
    - Self-justification and rationalization
    - General fear and anxiety
    - Other ______________________________

2. What behaviors do I recognize as telltale signs that I'm stuck? Is there a pattern of when it surfaces in my work, relationships, or schedule?
3. Where do I feel creative resistance in my body? How does it feel—physically, mentally, or emotionally? (See Feeling Words in the Appendix if you need help.)
4. What offers relief and allows me to return to creating again?
5. What is the difference between creative resistance and a creative block? Which do you struggle with most often? What form does it take?

MAKER PROMPT

Make something that represents the wholeness, balance, and irony of shalom that you use—or will use—to fight creative resistance.

Visio Divina

FOR CHAPTER 8

Elaine St. Louis, *Golden Bowl* (2017), oil on canvas, Denver, Colorado.

> Let the peace of Christ rule in your hearts, to which indeed you were called in one body; and be thankful. Let the word of Christ richly dwell within you, with all wisdom teaching and admonishing one another with psalms *and* hymns *and* spiritual songs, singing (*lit by His grace*) in your hearts to God. Whatever you do in word or deed, *do* all in the name of the Lord Jesus, giving thanks through Him to God the Father.
>
> **COLOSSIANS 3:15–17 (NASB 1995)**

READ.

Read the passage above from Colossians, focusing on the feelings and ideas it elicits.

REFLECT.

Consider the feelings and ideas that most stand out as you read the passage again. Underline and make note of your reflections.

REIMAGINE.

Does God really hear our prayers and praises? Yes, according to Scripture—our intercession and praise are the incense filling the golden bowls that surround His throne! The sweet aroma of our prayers and gratitude wafts in continuous waves of joy. For those who practice prayer and gratitude, the scent is recognizable oil that anoints and perfumes our lives. When thankfulness, grace, and His wisdom mark our lives, you and I shine!

In *Golden Bowl*, Elaine St. Louis provides a stunning depiction of our burning appreciation rising to God's heavenly place. As you take in the details of the painting, consider

- What is it that strikes you about this representation?
- Where is your attention drawn?
- What physical sensations does it elicit?
- Using your imagination, watch your dearest prayers rise with the smoke before God's throne. What sweet gift would you lift to God right now?
- Imagine the bowl is filled with your favorite aroma. Inhale that special scent with a deep breath. Name any feelings or emotions that arise.
- How many elements do you notice in the composition of this painting?
- If you removed one of them, how would the piece change? What does the Lord have to say to you about that?

RESPOND.

In what way does the work encourage you to respond in your life with God?

CHAPTER 8

THE LOST ART OF GRATITUDE

Have you ever gotten lost? I mean, really, *really* disoriented? Even with GPS today, it is possible.

One time (pre-GPS years), my brother Bob and I set off on a backpacking trip over the Continental Divide in Rocky Mountain National Park. He was nineteen years old and just home from his freshman year of college. I was seventeen and about to be a senior (if I lived that long). We intended to spend one night out and then hike down to meet friends at the cabin that had been in our family for many generations.

We had all the right equipment and provisions, including a good topo map we'd found at the cabin.

It was a steep climb—up and down. Setting off early from the trailhead, we climbed about 4,000 feet before pitching our tent in a windy and cold saddleback somewhere near 12,200 feet. As the sun dropped low in the sky, we bundled up to dine on trail mix and moderately warm ramen. Our campsite provided spectacular 360-degree views of the Twin Peaks Wilderness reflecting the warm palette of sunset. About 300 feet down a steep scree field, a high alpine lake reflected the late day colors like a mirror.

Tired and aware of a blustery cold front on the way, we went to bed early. Sometime in the middle of the night, a snow squall ripped the rainfly off our tent. Too cold to care, my brother and I stayed buried deep in our sleeping bags until morning.

The next day, we awoke with the sun, packed up, and began our descent to the lake.

Virtually no one makes it up to this lake so when we stopped briefly to fish, my brother caught five three-pound brown trout in less than thirty minutes. Huge wild strawberries and raspberry bushes heavy with fruit surrounded the lake. We grabbed some and kept going. Both of us knew we had a long day ahead. Little did we know how long!

Just past the lake, the trail descended sharply and narrowed to almost nothing. It had been decommissioned years before—meaning it was no longer maintained for backpackers like us.

Only animals and crazy people took this route! We, the crazies, forged on.

The way down was arduous. At one point, the mountain was so sheer and there were so many trees felled across the trail that we couldn't pass on foot. Instead, we had to tie our packs with a rope, lower them down over the logs before climbing over and dropping ourselves down.

We repeated this several times that hour.

A while later, as we hugged our packs in front of us to skirt a narrow, pine-packed ledge overlooking the ground thirty feet below, Bob realized the fish were too much weight to continue to carry for as long as we still had ahead of us. He dropped them over the edge.

Shortly after that, my brother tweaked his knee.

We finished our last bit of food—some now-smushed sandwiches, granola bars, and fruit—a little before the last rays of sun disappeared. Somehow, we were way behind schedule, but nightfall was right on time. It was cold, we were tired and hungry, and we still hadn't picked up the main trail. *Why was this taking so long?*, we both wondered. By flashlight, we tried our best to discern the difference between the old trail and the occasional deer trails we encountered. Around midnight, we hit the main trail. There, signs indicated we had *over thirteen miles to go* before we made it to the trailhead parking lot!

Comparing our map with the trail signs, we discovered what caused our miscalculation: our map was off by *nine* miles. (Are you KIDDING ME?!)

Bob and I connected the dots and realized the old map we'd been using must have belonged to one of our great-grandparents, and had most likely been made before aerial cartography was a thing—a significant thing.

Exhausted with still a long way to go, we stashed our packs off the side of the trail and literally limped the remaining distance. Some poor suckers—er, I mean, friends—would retrieve the packs for us later.

I've re-covered the mileage telling that story ever since.

Despite the beauty, the size of the fish, and some good memories with my brother, it was pretty scary and a painful experience. Thankfully, we found our way down—but it could have gotten dangerous very quickly.

As believers, I think we've been following a wonky map as well. Like our hiking fiasco, I believe our course has been dangerously off, the trail scaled to the wrong distance. As a result, the faith of too many people is defined by an overemphasis on heavy head knowledge, leading us to believe that in order to live the Christian life, all we have to do is study up and learn the lingo. The results have been scary. We have been way off, folks—especially when you consider how many people have left Christianity figuring Jesus' way wasn't leading to the life they had heard about.

Joyful, right-brain realities that surround a close relationship with Jesus have been displaced by ideas and infrastructure. Over time, attempting to find the trail of discipleship in this direction, each mile feels longer and more wearisome.

Indeed, if following Jesus truly is "about relationship and not religion," then why do so many churches and Bible studies push hard for information transfer? Why do they go limp when it comes to encouraging people with the vital truth, that a vibrant, transformed life with God and others is only sustainable if we—out of deep connection—are known?

Yes, I understand that being known is scary to some—maybe even most. But it is the trailhead for a life that is worth it. If we are serious about engaging our creativity for God's glory, you and I simply must learn how to get back to God's joy from the wilderness in which we've been wandering.

You Are Here

If you and I are following Jesus, joy is what fuels our journey homeward—not information or obligation. Joy is something you and I can never experience apart from our emotional right brain. Cultivating joyful creative practices encourages the growth of our capacity to demonstrate love, peace, patience, kindness, goodness, faithfulness, and self-control in our relationships. Our spiritual transformation depends on it.

This must become our main trail: following joy. How do we make a joyful, creative life that shines a bright light on God—the God who beams with delight when He looks at us? It starts with gratitude. We reflect Him. The world and our place within it are suddenly brighter.

Benefits of Gratitude

Practicing gratitude is one of the simplest ways to satiate our soul's need for joy. When you and I notice that we are joy-starved, gratitude is a low-hanging fruit snack along our way.

Counting our blessings is a good idea. Who knew? (Our grandmothers, that's who.) Today, neuroscience affirms that practicing gratitude encourages peace and connection within our mind, body, and spirit. When we feel "stuck," gratitude reorients our right brain—releasing a hit of dopamine and serotonin that leaves us feeling lighter and more positive. Tallying the many gifts we are blessed by moves our thinking from a scarcity and lack mindset to one of contentment and abundance.

Because our minds can't hold a positive and a negative thought simultaneously, a gratitude practice is a must. When we find ourselves stuck in a swirl of negativity, gratitude powerfully interrupts our discouraging ruminations. When you or I feel gratitude, it activates our limbic system—eventually grooving neuropathways in place that lead us back to joy. Our limbic system is the source of our emotional experiences and memory.

A thankful heart, soul, and mind set us up for delightful encounters. The mud of life is filtered away, allowing a clear stream of our identity to flow with delight in God and others. Acting with intention, directed focus, discretion, and skill, we are formed into the image of Jesus.

A preoccupation with good things in God's hands keeps our hearts and minds growing and maturing. Adopting a few regular practices—such as letting our heart savor experiences, creating a Gratitude List, journaling, sharing stories recapping our thankfulness, and meditating on the many good gifts we receive—"trains" the neuropathways of our brain in a thankful direction. The well-worn pathways in our brain establish habits—synapses that fire two hundred times faster than non-habitual reactions.

When gratitude becomes a habit, it gives us a pile of gifts, including:

- Improved overall health, including lower heart rate, inflammation markers, and blood pressure

- Relief from anxiety and depression
- More positive self-esteem
- Stronger relationships
- Less stress
- Greater resilience
- Increased joy and peace
- Deeper spiritual encounters
- Transforms our thinking from a mindset of scarcity and lack to one of contentment and abundance.

Gratitude also helps us connect with other people and God. It even helps us stay grounded in the present rather than become overcome with fearful thinking.

Let's look at each of these.

Connect with Others

Gratitude is another healing step toward the deep, genuine connection we desire with other people—a fundamental shift from individual awareness about ourselves to attunement with others. Attunement is the vital connection we make when you and I "tune in" to the emotions and experiences of others. We interact and synchronize—engaging and exchanging ideas, feelings, dreams, and needs.

Sharing what we are grateful for holds up a mirror for another—amplifying our gratitude imparts a little of our joy. Face to face with others, mirror neurons in our brain light up—resonating as you and I form and strengthen neuropathways of joy, discovering empathy and compassion.

A neuroscientific truism known as Hebb's Axiom states: "What fires together wires together." Through repeated use, synapses fire and form neuropathways. It's not so different from how relationships form, really—repeated joyful experience.

Hearing ourselves speak about a blessing received also does something to transform our hearts. We recognize its undeserved grace. Even if we don't share the same experiences, we are able to relate to one another more deeply. Gaining important understanding of one another this way, you and I form bonds. Over time, these bonds create the basis for belonging—an essential element in forming our identity. Who you and I ultimately become begins with the delight we share and enjoy with others. These healthy bonds strengthen our creative making.

Connect with God

When it comes to our relationship with God, gratitude plays a huge role. The point of a daily practice of gratitude is not to selfishly track what we have going for us but to further an awareness of our healthy attachment to One who wills our good and gives to us so lavishly.

God made every one of us as an expression of his love and pleasure—created out of His loving desire for connection with us. When we cultivate a daily practice of gratitude, we benefit in all the ways listed here, and, most importantly, you and I strengthen our connection with Him.

You and I become positively aware of God as the giver of all good things when we are grateful. The certainty that we aren't alone brings hope and improves our capacity to survive and adapt. Ultimately, it builds a sense of belonging and community.[15]

Cherish and enjoy the present

Finally, at any given moment, gratitude grounds us so that you and I can appreciate our most present reality—staving off fears that leak out in the form of our impatient future-casting, or haunting by past-tense stories.

This is not to say we live in Pollyanna-esque denial or toxic positivity. No. By learning to experience life in the joyful present, we make room for our souls to keep worries in perspective. When our souls orient around thankfulness, we stay alert, looking for what that something may be, even in the most challenging time. In-the-moment gratitude is the sure sign of a present heart.

Directing our thought-life to gratitude, you and I can't escape God's present, loving kindnesses in our lives, as Paul illustrated when he wrote, "Therefore, if you have been raised with Christ, keep seeking the things *that are* above, where Christ is, seated at the right hand of God. Set your minds on the things *that are* above, not on the things that are on earth" (Colossians 3:1–2 NASB). *This* is our starting point if we want to live an empowered life. Jesus' first disciples trained this way.

Shouldn't we?

Stay Humble

Gratitude offsets entitlement and pride. According to Andrew Murray,

> "When God created the universe, it was with the one objective of showing it in the glory of His love, His wisdom, and His power, and of making man the partaker of His perfection and blessedness. God wished to reveal Himself in and through created beings by communicating to them as much of His goodness and glory as they were capable of receiving. But this did not mean that man was given something that he could possess in itself, or a certain life or goodness that he could control and use whenever he wanted… Man's chief care, his highest virtue, and his only happiness, now and throughout eternity, is to

> present himself as an empty vessel in which God can dwell and manifest His power and goodness."[16]

A heart humbled by gratitude knows no shadow of entitlement or accolade. A grateful heart desires the glory of the One Who Gave before our life began. This puts the objective of our making in a whole new light, doesn't it? Yes! Enjoy these good gifts and celebrate them, remembering that their primary purpose is to glorify God and deepen your connection with Him.

How to Practice Gratitude

Start with the basics. Make a list. By writing down what we are thankful for, we focus on God's tangible goodness in our lives—the simple and the grand. I encourage journaling about each in detail, so they are easy to revisit at any time—prompting a sort of inner adoration for God's goodness and presence in our lives.

What can you journal about? Here are five topics to get you started: people, thin places, beauty, senses, and whispers from God. Let's take a look at each.

People

Ask yourself, *Who do I love that God has placed on my heart or in my path today?*

Here, we pay attention to who we love. Scripture makes it clear that God knew it wasn't good for us to be alone. So from the start, God didn't abandon Adam to an earthly life of physical isolation. He formed Eve so they could companion one another. No doubt, Adam was grateful for her! Well-modeled and designed by the Trinity, joy assures us that we are not alone.

Even though God is always with us and the Holy Spirit indwells us, we need face-to-face community.

So, who companions you? Specifically, what do you enjoy about them? What drew you to a relationship with that person? How do they make you feel—emotionally and physically?

Map out the details of some of your best memories together and include all your senses in the inventory. Who are some other gifts God has given you in human form? What is the best thing about them?

Especially if you often feel lonely or abandoned, reviewing the treasured ones on this list will surely remind you that *you are not alone*—quite the opposite. Here is proof that you enjoy others, and they enjoy you. (*Warm smile*)

Thin Places

Ask yourself, *Where do I feel most connected with God?*

Thin places are those mysterious environments where heaven seems to touch earth—where we readily sense the Lord's presence. Though the idea was made famous by Celtic Christians' ancient ruins and legendary landscapes that leaned themselves to divine mystery and worship, I believe each of us has thin places. There, we find memories, the anticipation of encounter, hope, and a sense of the holy. Some of the thin places where God meets with me include:

- Snuggled over coffee on a cool morning, watching sunbeams stream through the verdant shade that canopies our porch
- Standing near our cabin lakeshore where the cool, pinewood-and-water-spiced air hovers
- Walking a certain talcum powder-like Sarasota beach along the warm gulf surf line

- Lying in a mountain meadow, looking up at the stars twinkling in an inky, unpolluted night sky
- Making a lone, rolling, worshipful sweep down a Colorado ski run
- Sitting in the flutter-glistening gold of a rustling fall aspen grove

If a picture paints a thousand words, a thin place embodies the memory of a billion feels.

God's thick, available presence is predictable, time and time again in each set-apart place. Just writing about these now, I already feel my heart expanding. A spark of shalom ignites my soul again.

Biblically, God manifested such presence in the Garden of Eden with Adam and Eve, in a far-wilderness burning bush with Moses, for example, places that are revered today on any tour of the Holy Land. It seems likely that He would want to meet with us in the spaces we find sacred.

Where are yours? Where would you venture if you began to consider locations for your sacred opportunity? How would you linger?

Are you a beach person or a mountain type? Do you prefer the refresh of a rushing river or the splash of a lake? Sunrise or sunset? Stars or flowers? Desert or rainforest? Out of a loving desire for connection through all He created, God made every*thing* as an expression of his love and pleasure. Your leanings can uncover a lot about His unique love for you. What does it tell you about your love for Him?

Nature shouts the wonders of God's glory—encouraging us to notice and share an opportunity for common joy. Psalm 19:1–6 describes the active, worshipful role it plays in the world. When was the last time we paused to take note of this reality around us? Get in the habit of looking to see your surroundings.

The brilliance of God's creation echoes biblical metaphors that help us enjoy more of His Spirit in our lives—the light of day like the light of salvation; stars as our inheritance; waves, waterfalls, and oceans as objects of praise and glory; lion, lamb, horse as symbols of strength and victory.

Given "permission" to see God's revelation through our surroundings—without fear of being called deists or something worse—there is little we makers won't find wondrous. (Go ahead and Google "why is dirt amazing.") But to fan the flames of awe requires a curious spirit. You and I must get in the habit of taking time and looking closely. As believers, helping one another *see* beauty is part of our job description.

Senses

Ask yourself: *What am I experiencing right now through my five senses?*

Savoring what is taken in by our senses adds dimension to any gratitude practice. As you and I recognize sights, sounds, smells, textures, and tastes, our experiences in the moment, as well as the emotions and feelings they evoke, make our memories richer and more real to us. Identifying and labeling our experiences of such goodness help us recall special memories more easily. We are creating a treasure trove of gratitude for ourselves to recall on demand.

Did you know your sense of smell resides in your brain right next to your prefrontal cortex? It makes sense (literally) why the sense of smell embeds some of our most vivid memories. Similarly, rhythmic patterns of music and movement light up our brains more than almost anything as we listen and enjoy it. Aromas, songs, and sights entrench themselves.

When I was eleven, my mom was president of the Nebraska Wildlife Federation. Carnival midway music played off in the dusty distance as I sat beside her, leafing through the pages of *Ranger Rick Magazine* until kids would stop by our booth. When that happened, I got to hand out copies of the magazine and some stickers as my mom spoke with the parents. I remember feeling so proud of her and strangely empowered by the idea that I could help save endangered animals like the black-footed ferret or the whopping crane. We were on a mission together.

The scents of dust, straw, and corndogs in the heavy August air punctuated by the soundtrack for *Born Free* playing in our booth (in my grade-school mind, the music gave our Nebraska plains an African safari-like vibe. Cool.) To this day, I can tell you the groovy plaid swing top and jeans I was wearing. And when I smell corndogs, I feel the urge to croon.

Beauty

Ask yourself: *Where do I find beauty and what response does it evoke in my soul?*

Beauty means different things to different people, but one thing is sure: our souls both long for and testify to a universal need for beauty. Twentieth-century Swiss theologian and priest Hans Urs von Balthasar may have understood the concept best and most timelessly. He wrote, "Our situation today shows that beauty demands for itself at least as much courage and decision as do truth and goodness, and she will not allow herself to be separated and banned from her two sisters without taking them along with herself in an act of mysterious vengeance."[17]

Financial constraints aside, when the religious pendulum swung away from the artful crafting of cathedrals and toward today's strip mall and warehouse-style churches, I doubt anyone gave much thought to the cost Hans points out. Simply put, we cannot lose beauty without losing truth and goodness along with it—both aesthetically and spiritually. Somehow, we must welcome the transcendent nature of beauty back into the church narthex. We must curate a collection of beauty in our hearts and in our halls. Helping to bring the character of beauty back isn't optional for those who love Jesus. Apart from it, God's glory in our life and world cannot be adequately conveyed or enjoyed. Truth and goodness coexist—a chord of three strands. Appreciate what this "holy trinity" has to say daily.

In his book, *The Beauty Chasers: Recapturing the Wonder of the Divine*, Timothy Willard writes about how C. S. Lewis sparked his quest for beauty:

> "While Lewis wrote about the term *beauty*, the word he used to communicate an accurate biblical understanding of the word was *love*. But he didn't use the word *beauty* to only describe objects we find pleasing to the eye (aesthetics). Instead he described beauty as a staging point for something far bigger than mere aesthetic pleasure. Not the image of the galloping stallion but the quality of his movement. Not the 'dapple dawn drawn falcon' but the edge of love we feel when we witness its flight. For Lewis, beauty possesses a kind of magic that charges objects with visible delight. It also possesses a mysterious quality that invites the viewer to take up a quest."[18]

Beauty may be found in something aesthetically pleasing, but not necessarily so. Beauty embodies an enduring quality—a transcendent feeling.

To you, beauty may take the personal form of an act of kindness you witness, a good lyric that sways you, a striking mural that stirs something inside, or a Scripture aptly spoken over your circumstance. To me, it may be related to a joyful baby's giggle of discovery, the blossoming lives of our grown daughters, or observing the kindness and gentle humility my ninety-two-year-old dad demonstrates as he interacts with others who are younger. I often see beauty on a ski slope—in almost anything about the mountains. Such things easily arrest my mind. When the splendor of God strikes, it has the mystical ability to take my breath away and make my soul sing at the same time! Wherever we find it, beauty surrounds us every moment. These days, in a world full of ugly, you and I do well to enjoy what shimmers within our souls. These glimmers of God's goodness point us to what we hold sacred. In beauty, there is hope.

Whispers from God

Ask yourself: *How is God speaking to me?*

The Bible tells us Elijah the prophet did not hear Him through the drama of hurricane-force winds, an earthquake, or fire. Nope. It was a still, small voice that got his attention (1 Kings 19:11–13). I think most of us are more like Elijah than we realize. We just need to listen better.

Why does a whisper entice our attention? A soft voice hints at the power of a secret exchange. The still small voice Elijah encountered caused him to cover his face. Within the burning bush, the voice called Moses to remove his sandals. Supernatural or routine, God is speaking. I believe God speaks words over us all the time—through ordinary things, people, our surroundings, and His Word. Are you and I on our toes—shoes off, aware, and expecting opportunities of divine exchange?

He sings over us tenderly, graciously in the background music of our days—highlighting moments, people, and significant opportunities for connection with Him. The better we recognize God's part in these, the more our hearts expand with thanksgiving. Even when life's storms hit us—and they will—you and I will better hear His voice because we have been practicing.

Gratitude makes us brave. Courageous gratitude helps us remember that we are not alone—and have never been. We create best from a place of connection. God is with us in *everything*.

Through His whispers, God may invite us into a conversation. Sometimes those conversations inspire action. His power always manifests a connection with His glory. That glory is ours to reflect in humble gratitude.

Jesus said to his disciples, "There is so much more I would like to say to you, but it's more than you can grasp at this moment. But when the truth-giving Spirit comes, he will unveil the reality of every truth within you. He won't speak on his own, but only what he hears from the Father, and he will reveal *prophetically* to you what is to come. He will glorify me on the earth, for he will receive from me what is mine and reveal it to you" (John 16:12–14 TPT).

Creating space to listen to God's whispers, our voice becomes less important to us. We learn to hang, even more gratefully, on His every word.

By thoroughly tracking the dimensions of our daily gratitudes, you and I remember them to scale. Most importantly, the practice of gratitude maps our way back to joy when we've been wandering lost. Revisiting the good gifts we have been given by God and one another reminds us that we are not alone on this trek. His joy is our shared strength and truly something for which to we can be grateful (Nehemiah 8:10).

MAKER'S AFFIRMATION

Makers keep grace-based bearings—spontaneously expressing their undeserved blessings and sharing treasures gifted to them by God.

I am a maker.

Maker Exercises

QUIETING

In the Psalms we are told, "Be still and know that I am God. . . The Lord Almighty is with us; the God of Jacob is our fortress" (Psalm 46:10–11 niv). However, being still is often easier said than done. Nonetheless, God says it and our brain, body, and soul need it!

Sometimes our feelings overwhelm us. Other times, we find ourselves "unplugged" from our emotions, circumstances, and relationships. These are signs of emotional dysregulation. Learning to become aware of our feelings helps to integrate both sides of our brain. This kind of regulation serves our relationships and creativity. But what if we find it hard to reconnect? By learning how to recognize our body's fear response, you and I can take steps to soothe ourselves and settle down our emotions. Then we will automatically become more clear about our identity, empathetic toward others, and able to remain relationally connected.

Polyvagal nerve stimulation is one soothing method aimed at calming our vagus nerve. While there are many ways to go about it, we will talk about how to soothe our discomfort by tapping. Tapping certain pressure points helps stimulate the vagus nerve and "recalibrates" involuntary functions of the autonomic nervous system—things like our heart rate, breathing, gut, and voice. This helps us settle down. To try it, follow these instructions:

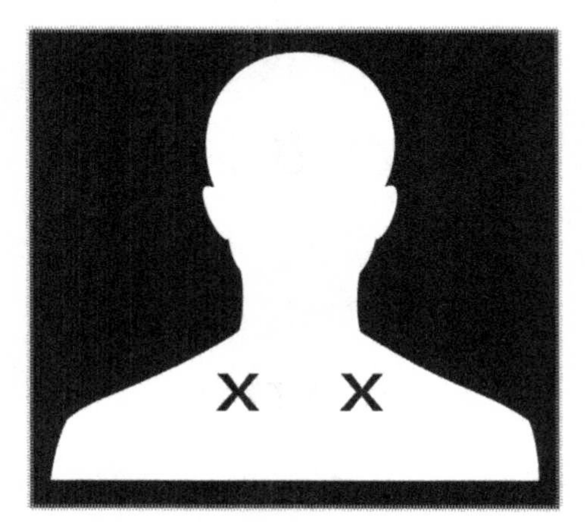

- **Locate the tapping points.** Using the third and fourth fingers on each hand, locate the notch in your neck—below the chin and between your collar bones. Each tapping point is approximately one inch below the notch and one inch either side.
- **Begin tapping as you breathe in.** There, at the pace of your heartbeat, tap firmly (but not so much that it hurts) and rhythmically, breathing in through your nose as you tip your head back a little. Slightly increase the speed of your tapping as your belly fills with air.
- **As you breathe out, rub the same spot.** Once you have taken a full breath, begin to rub the same spots as you slowly exhale through your mouth.
- **Repeat for four breaths.**
- **Quieted?** When you have completed the sequence, take one more deep breath as you quietly consider whether your body and emotions feel quieted. If not, repeat.

Note: Some enjoy adding breath prayer to the breathing pattern. Such as, "The Lord is my shepherd. I have everything I need," or "When I am afraid, I will trust in you, Lord."

GRATITUDE

Gratitude is a powerful practice. (You've probably noticed from practices in the previous chapters.) Brené Brown discovered the relationship between gratitude and joy. A renowned shame researcher, leadership consultant, and author, Brown enlisted a qualitative research method known as "Grounded Theory" to conduct more than 10,000 interviews with people of all ages all around the country asking two main questions:

1. What is the anatomy of human connection?
2. How does it work?

These questions led her—a self-proclaimed "story catcher"—to more questions, but the sum of her research surfaced a key finding of special interest to us. People who were living the most "wholehearted" lives—lives deemed resilient and inspiring by the research—were those who had learned the superpower of embracing their imperfections and vulnerabilities.

As she dug even deeper into the research, it turned out that these same folks valued and crafted their resilient lives around similar practices. Many of these practices—including gratitude and creativity—leapt from her data. And when it came to gratitude, she found something truly incredible. She writes, "Without exception, every person I interviewed who described living a joyful life or who described themselves as joyful actively practiced gratitude and attributed their joyfulness to their gratitude practice." Their practices included things like keeping gratitude journals, doing daily gratitude meditations or prayers, creating gratitude art, and stopping during their busy days to acknowledge their gratitude out loud.[19]

NOW IT'S YOUR TURN

Choose the version of gratitude practice that you've enjoyed so far. Because morning and evening are highly neurologically formational times for our brain, I suggest implementing your gratitude practice at one or the other. Grab your Gratitude List and reflect on your answers to the following questions.

- What person, place, thing, or experience are you especially grateful for right now?
- Describe in detail the circumstances that shine when you think about your gratitude, including as much detail and insight as possible.
- Why is the timing of this memory significant at this point in your life? What brought it to mind?
- When you reflect on the memory, what is God revealing about Himself through the object of your gratitude?
- Listen for His response. Take time to prayerfully interact with Him. What does He think about the memory you are enjoying?

REFLECTION

1. Have you experienced God leading you through joy (a sense that He is delighted that you two are together)?
2. In addition to your sense of thankfulness, are you conscious of how God's glory transcends each thing you are grateful for?
3. Do you regularly talk about the things you are grateful for with others who are close to you?
4. Do you expect and listen for God's voice? Where do you feel most connected with God?
5. What are you experiencing through your senses that makes you thankful?
6. Where do you find beauty, and what response does it evoke in your body and soul?
7. How does God speak to you? Is it a whisper? A shout? A gesture? A sign? A question?

MAKER'S PROMPT

Make something to bless someone you care about—just because. Then, give your creation to that person.

Visio Divina

FOR CHAPTER 9

Julie McKnight, *Aslan's Tale* (2017), composite digital art, Victor, Idaho.

Listen, my people, to my instruction;
Incline your ears to the words of my mouth.
I will open my mouth in a parable;
I will tell riddles of old,
Which we have heard and known,
And our fathers have told us.
We will not conceal them from their children,
But we will tell the generation to come the praises of the LORD,
And His power and His wondrous works that He has done.

PSALM 78:1–4 NASB

READ.

Read through Psalm 78:1–4. Take in the true story for a minute or two. Allow it to speak to your heart.

REFLECT.

Read the passage again, slowly, and highlight anything that draws your attention.

In the Bible, Jesus is called the Lion of Judah, referring to His absolute authority and power. This Lion is also the Lamb of God, gentle and meek enough to go to the slaughter for our less-than-perfect stories.

Our stories are part of God's. In His, He proves himself a storyteller, a foreteller, and a truth-teller. All of Scripture encompasses those things. Beyond being our savior, Jesus rejoices in the good and ugly that you and I overcome *by His grace.*

That's it in a nutshell: our story is grace.

The best wisdom we glean results at the intersection of God's truth and who we, *indeed, imperfectly* are. He promises never to leave or forsake us—which has nothing to do with our personal performance (Deuteronomy 31:8). Because we are like Him, we are storytellers.

Becoming who you and I are made to be means we embrace the account of our life before Him and close others—to know ourselves and to be known. We integrate our embodied experiences—attachments, emotions, physical and mental sensations—as part of our spiritual practice as God secures our identity. In telling our story, we reflect on our family history, relationships, life events, and His Word to clarify and pass on authentic, hard-won wisdom and grace to future generations.

REIMAGINE.

Count on Him to make you brave as you tenderly overlay your own story on Julie McKnight's amazing digital piece, *Aslan's Tale.*

- Once again, take in the whole storybook scene. Make room in your heart to imagine yourself in the scene without agenda.
- What are you drawn to overall?
- Where are you in the painting?
- How do you feel about the image? Consider your body, breath, and emotions. Assign one word or feeling to capture your overall impression.
- What story does it tell you?
- Does it make you curious? (Prayerfully interact with God about your questions.)
- How would you write the rest of the story?

RESPOND.

Bring the story alive. Share your insights with someone close—engaging them with animation, emotion, feeling words, imagery, and gesture. (Leave out any impulse to overexplain, justify your understanding, or provide a backstory.) Encourage them to just listen to the goodness of God in your words.

CHAPTER 9

YOUR STORY MATTERS

"There is the 'you' that people see and then there is the 'rest of you.' Take some time and craft a picture of the 'rest of you.' This could be a drawing, in words, even a song. Just remember that the chances are good it will be full of paradox and contradictions.

– BRENNAN MANNING, *THE FURIOUS LONGING OF GOD*

There I was at thirty-four years old, sitting in a semicircle of women of various ages ranging from the midtwenties to midseventies. The ten of us had signed up for a two-semester Bible study based on the book *Sacred Romance* by John Eldredge and Brent Curtis. According to the cover copy, we were about to find ourselves immersed in the love story of the Lord's wild and beautiful wooing of us, and in the process be captured by the desire for our First Love. *Sounds compelling,* I thought. As the mom of two grade-school girls, and an avid reader of heady, evangelical Christian "how-to" literature, the idea of Jesus as the lead in a romance with me held curious appeal.

That is, until our group leader, Sandy, explained that before our study was over we would each be given time—an entire evening—to tell our life story. At that point, my blood went cold.

Nice meeting you, ladies. Gotta go!

You see, over the years, I'd learned that sharing my stuff was usually a bad idea. I'd learned this thanks to well-intentioned but emotionally immature friends, the Christian rumor mill, family interactions, and the misguided nature of many "accountability groups." As a result, I'd come to believe that my life, my "issues," and my gifts were either not enough, or else they were way too much. In different situations with various people, I felt as though the pages of my story had been wadded up and tossed in the garbage. Too often, sharing my story had ended with hot, stinging tears of bewilderment and betrayal. Better just keep things to myself. To tell my *whole* story—the *real* one—would only further confirm my worst fears about myself.

What I Really Needed

What I needed was what we all need—a trusted friend who could also serve as a gracious and loving "editor." Our editor friends are those who see us with God's eyes of grace, help us remember where we are in the plotline, and lovingly remind us who we truly are in unique and personal ways. This kind of close other comes alongside to help us rewrite where our story has gone wrong. In doing so, they call us out and beckon us back to God's better story—the one that down deep we all want to tell.

Up to that point, I'd never had a friend who had helped me lovingly edit my personal narrative, and in my opinion, they are far too rare. Yet, if you and I practice any breed of creativity, we'd best have this kind of friend in tow.

Do you have trustworthy editors? People who set you free from hurtful lies and turn your attention to more important things above (Colossians 3)? We collect stories throughout our lives that influence our making. Is there anyone who helps you stay grace-brave enough to tell your whole story? Grace-bravery springs from unconditional love and joy of relationship. For most of us, it takes this "Jesus with skin on" friendship for the reality of His story to finally integrate with ours. If you and I don't have two to three close spiritual friends with whom we can share our stories (and who can share their stories with us), our spiritual growth is at stake.

Ideally, these friends are part of our church. They are people we interact with, every few days at least. And ideally, we can identify and connect with them sooner in our lives than later. But wherever and whenever friends like these come into our lives (I was thirty-four the first time I experienced the power of my need to know and be known in this way), it's a game-changer.

This is the power of story in our lives. This is the headspace for healthy, courageous creative freedom!

Careful Curiosity

Being vulnerable enough to weave our story into our work does not mean you and I are signing up for judgment, rebuke, instruction, critique, or correction *unless we ask for it.* It also doesn't mean our story is there for others to gossip about, though not everyone is mature enough to know better.

Our stories reveal cracks in our once "well-polished" images. As these flaws become visible to one another, you and I must be mindful to untangle any inclination we may have toward control or superiority. Trusting someone with our story is a powerful experience. It has the power to either encourage our soul to come out in the open more often or affirm its existence hidden in the wilds of loneliness. Weakness is nothing short of courage.

As artists, you and I know that everything we make embodies a little part of us and our story. We pat our narrative on its lil behind as we nudge it out on stage in front of others, hoping the world will be tender toward it and help it grow. Our hope is that people will get curious enough to ask questions, to know us through our little one.

Similarly, when you and I meet people whose stories or opinions are vastly different from our own, we can cultivate common ground by digging for our own curiosity and asking questions to understand more about them. In the process, we help them become more whole, just as they help us become more whole when they are curious—and not judgmental—about our work.

You and I have a choice to meet sincere and curious questions with authentic answers.

Brené Brown says, "Vulnerability sounds like truth and feels like courage. Truth and courage aren't always comfortable, but they're never weakness."[20] From the sounds of it, living curiously is the way to go if we want to avoid judgmentalism.

Seeking to know one another, we encourage the beautiful incarnation of our inner landscape. As we look for reflections of God and ourselves in the stories of others, we build our capacity for awareness and attunement. Shared stories help us develop trust, freedom, and authenticity together—along with a deeper sense of purpose.

In her book, *Walking on Water: Reflections on Faith and Art,* Madeline L'Engle writes:

> "Stories are able to help us to become more whole, to become Named. And Naming. God asked Adam to name all the animals, which was asking Adam to help in the creation of their wholeness. When we name each other, we are sharing in the joy and privilege of incarnation, and all great works of art are icons of Naming.

> "When we look at a painting or hear a symphony or read a book and feel more Named, then, for us, that work is a work of Christian art. . . We can know only if it speaks within our own hearts and leads us to living more deeply with Christ in God."[21]

We learn about grace in God's Word, but pragmatically we need one another (especially people who are different from us) to experience and grow in this grace. Everyone needs people of grace who can encourage us to sort out and share our authentic—sometimes messy—stories.

Coauthors of Identity

Our lives are not secrets to be kept. They are testimonies of God. When you share *your* story, it inspires and changes *my* story. In reciprocal, interactive ways, we are coauthors in a mutual story. Creatively, we write on the souls of one another—growing our individual identities and transforming our spiritual lives. Sharing stories, we learn to attune and empathize with one another. We share a wealth of wisdom, power, acceptance, and joy, becoming richer all the while.

Seeing and being seen, we catch stories and release them in community, a process that heals us little by little. We feel it in our bones as stories form us. Our souls relax—living in the skin of newfound wholeness and acceptance. The resulting bonds formed between us are life- changing—defining who we are in God's grace. Together, we are coauthors in our becoming.

But we must be careful. In light of the power they hold, stories can transform us for better or worse. It's a big responsibility to respectfully hold someone's history. And let's be honest, occasionally we will disappoint one another. Trust me, our growth is worth the mistakes we may make. That, too, is part of our story.

The Benefits of Story

When it comes to brain benefits, stories deliver! They have been proven a powerful delivery mechanism to

- Help memory
- Increase attention
- Improve our capacity to listen
- Spark imagination
- Create visualizations
- Eliminate stress
- Encourage presence in the moment

A thoughtful story can inspire teamwork, establish understanding despite differences, foster empathy, build trust, deliver hard truths, and help us examine our values and motivations—all while capturing our attention with its narrative!

Most importantly, our story can show people Jesus in a relatable and memorable way.

It's How We Think

Have you ever thought about why Jesus taught in parables? Because He knew what neurobiologists and story scientists (yes, they exist) can now prove beyond a shadow of a doubt: we think in story. Our brain is biologically wired for it. Though our core motivations differ, story is our shared heartbeat. In addition, you and I will scan the skies and beat the bushes until we find a good story we can live in.

Ask any developmental learning expert and they will agree that, when you are delivering information to an audience, these stats apply:

- Roughly 40 percent will be visual learners (learn best through video, diagram, or illustration)

- Roughly 40 percent will be auditory learners (learn best through lecture and discussion)
- Roughly 20 percent will be kinesthetic learners (remember best through emotional connections and feelings)

Can you guess what effectively reaches *all* these learning types? Yep. One hundred percent learn best through well-crafted stories that creatively spark our imagination, emotion, senses, and memory.

His- (and Her-) Story

In cultures around the world predating language and the written word, story has been the primary means of passing down important history, facts, instruction, ritual, societal expectations, lessons on morality, wisdom, and more. For thousands of years, stories and sacred texts were *told* to people listening in community—not *read* quietly and alone. We started off together. That should tell us something.

Historically, we search for connection. In the age of enlightenment, Industrial Revolution, and most recently the digitization of our world, the search for connection seems to have become more desperate. Conversations that were once opportunities to build bridges have been bombed out by cancel culture, agendas, and us-versus-them thinking. And in the process, what is becoming abundantly clear is that people aren't built for isolation. We can't replace personal relationships and stories with social media, screens, and a 24/7 news cycle. Our beings cannot be inoculated against the resulting loneliness and anxiety.

Storytelling is an art and an antidote for what ails us. It narrows the gap between us. Some people are true artists at *telling* theirs, I *write* or *paint* mine. Every day, I come up with rewrites, do-overs, and second thoughts—chicken scratching through my mistakes to make a better draft. Rarely is what first comes out of my mouth (or computer or canvas) as articulate as I wish it were. Yet I know my story is important to tell.

But the process is diminished when I don't share my story.

Our art *is* our story. Whatever we make with our life is our medium. The unique creativity we possess and express reveals things about us that help us become more of who we are meant to be. We need story-laden interaction with one another to help us discover ourselves. Unstoried is unknown. And, when you and I remain unstoried, we remain less integrated as people—unidentified and without identity.

Our Brain on Story

Scientists tell us we have a neural story net. This is a region toward the back of our brain that, as we listen to a story, is hard at work processing that story. Well-told, a story that we connect with will make sense to us and others, be meaningful enough to hold our interest, and capture our emotion. When all is said and done, if we personalize what we've heard, it will influence us going forward. If you and I receive a story and make it our own, specific regions of our brain light up. Fascinatingly, these are the same regions that light up in the brain of the person telling the story! In other words, we imagine ourselves living their experience. Mirror neurons in our brain fire in the same sequence as those occurring in the brain of the person telling the story. Our behaviors and communication "tune us in" to one another. This is called "synchronization."

Regardless of what we are making as creators, we must remember this: stories give us the best chance of influencing others. "Facts never saved anyone," as they say. That includes faith- based facts. While we are never promised that our words, moves, or images will open the door to life change for someone else, our stories help crack it at least. A crack is all that's needed to let the light of God shine from inside us—spreading the influence of our story.

Well-told stories are deeply etched into our memories. These memories are stored in our hippocampus, and our hippocampus loves a good story. Here, our brain readily tells and keeps the ones that have a strong overarching narrative—especially ones which resonates with our beliefs and values. Even if a story does not align with our ideas, our brain hangs onto it, creating an opportunity for us to begin to soften toward those new ideas.

This is why, as makers, if we want to influence people, our best chance at fostering lasting understanding and empathy will be found in a narrative space—not a debate. Within our brain, empathy is key to creating resolution. Add the resulting comfort of compassionate action steps and we've got a cultural best seller. That's influence!

Engagement, personal relevance, and influence demonstrate the power our individual stories hold. Stories create relationships, and relationships influence our identity.

It used to be thought that our brains quit growing once we mature into adulthood. But current science has proven that our brains continue to grow and change throughout our lives *in the context of vibrant relationship*. The Word of God in the context of relationship has the same effect on our spiritual growth. Now more than ever it is clear: we have the capacity to help grow one another as we are known through life's ups and downs.

The deep connection of knowing and being known is the same attachment love the disciples had with Jesus and between themselves as followers. It is the same love that modern-day disciples can experience. Jesus knows us all, inside out. He longs for us to understand that it is His choice to be with us despite the secret parts of our stories that make us cringe.

Everything we love most tells the story of God in some way. When you and I are making—whatever that means for us—we aren't just making. We are making God known within our story. For His glory, it is important that we allow the Holy Spirit to search and guide the motivations, thoughts, implications, and messages we share.

The truth of our story—not the perfect version but the *real* one—transcends image. As a result of its telling, we are more fully known. Being known is an essential step toward unleashing identity, establishing community, and building belonging. Most importantly, the freedom to tell our story is a sure sign of grace at work in our lives and relationships.

Pearls

No one really likes plastic pearls.

Most of us prefer what is *real.*

True masters of story have reckoned with what is fake in the mess of their backstory. For all of us, our backstory refines the character our lives reflect. The creative twists and turns of our story communicate our soul's journey. Below a conscious level, the tools of honest emotion, senses, and experiences string together like pearls. You and I create beauty from what was once sandy grit, as the strand of our making is threaded. Lacing bits of our story into what we make, it becomes transformational—less transactional. We release God's goodness in our creating and character.

Examining What Motivates Our Making

We may not even realize when it is happening, but sometimes fear gets the better of us despite our beliefs and deep-seated desire to be known. Remember the fear-based motivations we learned earlier from author and community-building expert Ed Khouri? When these unhealthy and masked motivations underlie our storyline, our true self fades into shadows of fear-based behaviors and our false self.[22] Somehow, we end up posing as someone we are not—thereby derailing opportunities for deep connection. Subconsciously, we allow fear to outweigh our *godly* motivations and we attach ourselves to what is fake.

Given the opportunity to make ourselves known, it's important that we check ourselves for misleading motivations. In such moments these drives reveal our authenticity—or lack of it. Impure motives have a way of leaking out—undermining trust and exposing our greatest attachments. If we share a story, are you and I doing so out of a desire for deep connection with God and connection with those who are listening, or are we self-protecting? If we feel seen, safe, soothed, and secure with God, there is a story to be told.

Telling our own stories and *connecting* with one another's stories give us a solid opportunity to influence—and be influenced by—the identity and spiritual growth of one another.

Telling Our Stories to Ourselves

Each of us has a story. *Once upon a time*. . .The End.

Hardly satisfying. Everything in between is what matters.

So, what goes in the middle?

What are you and I making with the unique, creative life we've been given?

Will what we are doing matter in eternity?

Before you scurry down a rabbit hole of weighty thoughts, don't think about these questions as a heavy burden. Instead, consider them as the way life should be. Telling our stories is an invitation to appreciate our God-led adventure. Our stories give our gratitude context. For some of us, this changes our perspective on all we have lived up to this point—not to mention our outlook on what comes next.

In our making, you and I examine and reveal our narratives—some of which aren't true. Storytelling forces us to look more closely at the investment of our words, work, and relationships. Every day when you and I look back over the hours, what story are we writing/painting/marketing/raising/sculpting/scripting/building/scoring? What story did we tell?

Creating a life worth living takes bravery—not to mention the guidance of Holy Spirit. Authenticity requires courage—the habit of meeting danger without fear—as we draft a day's story. Brave ones speak of their experiences because they are free. All of us need to fight for such freedom. Comprised of good decisions and poor, triumphs and weaknesses in relationships and faith, these grace-brave souls are not afraid to be known—they know they must. Deep acquaintance with self and God's grace make their biographies supremely beautiful. Secure in who they are—and are becoming—brave creators invite us to tell our own true-life tales. Or at least start thinking about it. . .

It may be contrary to common sense, but our weaknesses and vulnerabilities are actually the strength of our lives—they connect us. Making us relatable and in need of a savior, our failings and flaws crack us open and give God all the more room to shine. By learning to tell our story in close community, you and I realize the transformative spiritual discipline of knowing and being known. We realize something more powerful than the fear of having our greatest weaknesses, screw-ups, and sins exposed. We exchange shameful narratives for a taste of the unequaled, special delight, appreciation and acceptance God promises us.

Yes. It's risky. But the only way you and I get better at telling stories is to tell them. The truth is, my life is no fairytale but neither is it a horror novel. Before I let others in on its secret highs and lows,

I didn't appreciate the rich goodness that my story reveals. The central lines thread together my desperate need for a savior, accentuating God's lovingkindness and mercy along the way. His character in my life is the result of the people, hard-fought battles, first-hand truths, and in hindsight, a redeeming plot. Yours is, too.

"Naked and unashamed," our tenderness to weakness benefits the formation of spiritual muscle within the body. You and I connect and integrate emotions, relationships, identity, logic, and skill—making each other stronger and even more brave. We become change-makers in each other's lives.

MAKER'S AFFIRMATION

Makers testify with the stories they tell and the transformational life they live.

I am a maker.

Maker Exercises

QUIETING

Color reflects light to varying degrees, but that's not all. Did you know that red makes your heart beat faster? Blue light sets the "inner clock" of our circadian rhythms—even in non-sighted people. As a color, it is known to calm. Color does things to our subconscious. For example, color and light can affect our mood, heart rate, blood pressure, alertness, and impulsiveness. Light levels also affect us by stimulating our hypothalamus to release hormones. These hormones induce sleep, wakefulness, body temperature, and other circadian responses.

1. Close your eyes and take a few deep breaths.
2. Check in with your heart. How are you doing?
3. With a Sharpie, draw a large rectangle on your paper. Then, draw a line down the center vertically and equal horizonal sections across the rectangle to create six boxes of equal size.

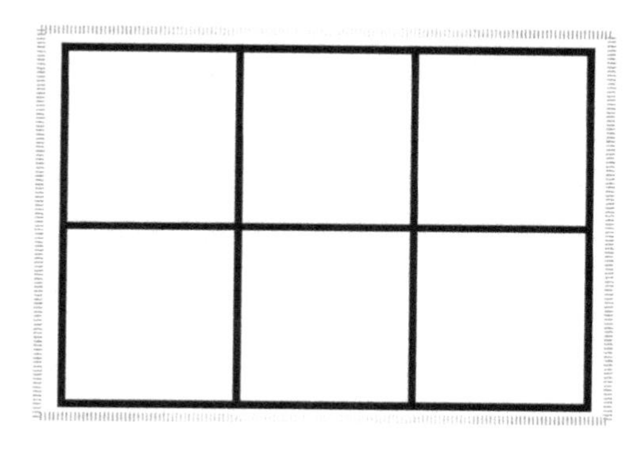

1. Choose a color that represents your mood right now. Consider how intense (light or dark) this feels. In color theory, this is called "value." In the first box, demonstrate the color of your mood and its value.
2. In the second box, using the same color and value, add texture to convey how this physically feels (for example, bristly, soft, flowing, sharp, bumpy). Take a minute to imagine how it feels in your body.
3. Pick three more emotions. In three boxes, recall the feeling and repeat the process of matching a color, value, and texture that communicates what you remember. If it helps, reflect on the specific circumstances involved.
4. Before you color in the last box, take a moment to be quiet again. Close your eyes and breathe a few deep, slow breaths. As you do, think about Jesus and how He feels about you. What color is His feeling for you? What intensity does it convey? Is there a texture to it? Once you can feel the color, value, and texture of Jesus' love and compassion, fill in the last box accordingly.

GRATITUDE

Ask God to bring to mind someone who has played a significant, positive, impactful role in your life—someone who still inspires you and makes you feel special. Picture that person sitting with you right now. Feel the warmth and comfort of their presence. Look in their eyes. What is the expression on their face? What would you want to tell them about their significance to you if they were actually there? Thank the Lord for them. Praise Him for who He created. When you have time, send that person a heartfelt note of appreciation. Copy the words to your Gratitude List.

REFLECTION

1. What narrative(s) (negative thought patterns) work against your joy?
2. Do you have a trustworthy "editor friend" who can help you get free from such lies and establish God's truth about who you are?
3. Are you curious about other people's stories? Why or why not?
4. If you are honest, when you disagree with someone, do you get curious, aggressive, or just write them off?
5. How does your creativity communicate joy or foster understanding?
6. In God's story, will what we are making matter?

MAKER'S PROMPT

Make something that reminds you of your rootedness in God.

Visio Divina

FOR CHAPTER 10

Debra Komodore, *Walking on Water* (2023), mixed media, Denver, Colorado.

READ.

Read the following verses aloud to discover their meaning.

> She is clothed in strength and dignity,
> and she laughs without fear of the future.
>
> **PROVERBS 31:25 NLT**

REFLECT.

Proverbs 31 is not just for women. (Scripture often personifies wisdom as female.) With that in mind, reread Proverbs 31:25, circling any words or phrases that jump out at you.

REIMAGINE.

When you're ready, turn your attention to *Walking on Water* by Debra Komodore. Now, consider the passage in the context of the piece. Ask the Lord to guide your reimagining.

- What do you notice? (Consider the whole composition, mood, and any feelings it evokes.)
- Ask the Lord to help you feel what the artist is representing. What bobs to the surface of your attention?
- Who or what does the flamingo seem to embody?

This summer, I have been "stalked" by flamingos. Flamingos are flocking to me in Hobby Lobby, airport shops, malls, restaurants, Home Depot, a neighbor's yard art, and even across the hall from my dad's retirement community apartment! I've mentioned it to some friends, including Debra Komodore. She's witnessed some of these "pop-up appearances" with me recently.

Like all of us, Debra has a story. The details are not necessary. A professional installation artist and teacher, she is coming out of a long season of darkness that progressively shut down her creativity—it was as if the life force of her faith and joy were being slowly strangled.

Wisely and without wallowing, Debra sat with God in her circumstances and emotions—seeking, asking, and listening to the guidance of the Word and Lord. Eventually, she wrestled through. It took a while, but the sun came out. Now, accepting an invitation to freedom, joy, and peace, Debra is convinced that God is inviting her and all of us to come out in the sunshine and play.

When I mentioned that I struggled to find the art for this chapter, she created *Walking on Water*. (Note: "cartoonish style" is not her typical genre.) She had just returned from a waterskiing week in the mountains with family—something she enjoys every other week during the summer. The combination of speed and sunshine creates a happy place—whether on water or snow! She says being on skis keeps her in the present, NOW—most alive. It also serves as a reminder: if God can change molecules to walk on water, He can change our circumstances instantly. What a wonder!

Her mixed media work is a playful nod to my flamingo encounters and a celebration of the sunshine of God that has dawned again in her life. Even in the intensity of her dark season, God grew her into the awareness that strength and dignity are a choice. Play is necessary for the joy all of us need to make good choices. Debra anticipates opportunities for spiritually transforming play every day. Do we?

RESPOND.

Making invites play. Prayerfully respond to the Lord about your interaction with His Word and the mixed media art. Journal your responses.

- What wisdom do you see in play?
- Today, what sunshine and laughter does it invite in your life with God and others? Make a plan to play.
- Thank God for His faithfulness to meet you on the playground.

CHAPTER 10

FUN AND THE SERIOUS NATURE OF PLAY

"Serious art is born from serious play."
– JULIA CAMERON, *THE ARTIST'S WAY: A SPIRITUAL PATH TO HIGHER CREATIVITY*

Over the years, I've worked with many people and researched lots of topics in the fields of spiritual formation, neuroscience, and creativity. Usually, I have been more student than expert, so every time I had a lightbulb moment—a new connection, or a geek-out thrill in a conversation—my reaction was always THAT'S SO FUN, RIGHT?! Each time that happened, more often than not, I'd look to whomever I was working with for a signal of affirmation.

Frequently, I was met with a head tilt and blink of confusion. *Fun?* they seemed to wonder.

Yes. Fun! Bringing ideas/things/materials/processes/people together in new ways is fun.

Inherently, you and I crave our own version of variety, novelty, challenge, and adventure.

Honestly, who doesn't love fun? As part of the Trinity, Jesus certainly does. After all, creating the universe must have been a blast—and each new day a recreational exercise. As mentioned before, we are made in the Trinitarian image and fun is part of our joyful identity.

In my opinion, Jesus' popularity among the outcast—partiers, prostitutes, wealthy tax collectors, and the lot—implies he wasn't some stuffy religious killjoy. His parties must have been fun for this crowd of followers because they wanted to be around Him.

I imagine that He invited everyone. Can't you see His warm, grace-filled smile welcoming them at the door? I'm guessing that the wine he poured was the best vintage, the water more refreshing after a wholehearted dance of the hora. I'll bet they played some version of cornhole, too, and that He served more than enough loaves of the best homemade bread and the freshest Galilean daily catch—sending his guests home full and satisfied.

What we do know for sure is that people of legendary worldliness found a savior whose way of life was more compelling than their own. The Messiah they had been waiting for embodied a goodness, grace, and *joi de vivre* they hadn't expected.

Researching her latest book, *The Power of Fun: How to Feel Alive Again,* science journalist Catherine Price affirms that we all could use more fun. She proposes that you and I must look for opportunities that provide us with a sense of these three things: playfulness, connection, and flow. To me this describes every creative venture—especially, those with God.

And it also provides us a head start on a keen definition of play.

So, why is it hard to imagine play as an important spiritual discipline?

What Is Play?

According to Dr. Stuart Brown, the guy who quite literally wrote the book on it—which he entitled *Play*—our need for play is as important as sleep—neither of which most of us get enough of. In addition to being an author, Dr. Brown is also a physician, psychiatrist, and founder of the

National Institute for Play. He resists limiting the word *play* to a single definition, instead directing our focus to its characteristics. Anything with the following traits qualifies as play:

- Purposeless (done for its own sake)
- Voluntary
- All-consuming
- Holds inherent attraction (it's fun, exciting, and makes you feel good)
- Offers improvisational potential (serendipitous; not rigid in form)
- Provides freedom from a sense of time
- Diminishes consciousness of self
- Something we want to keep doing[23]

In addition, Brown notes:

> "Authentic play comes from deep down inside us. It's not formed or motivated solely by others. Real play interacts with and involves the outside world, but it fundamentally expresses the needs and desires of the player. It emerges from the imaginative force within. That's part of the adaptive power of play: with a pinch of pleasure, it integrates our deep physiological, emotional, and cognitive capacities. And quite without knowing it, we grow. We harmonize the influences within us. Where we may have felt pulled in one direction by the heart and another direction by the head, play can allow us to find a balanced course or a third way."[24]

Play integrates all aspects of our being, starting with the right side of the brain. Surprised? Our intellect, body, and emotions coregulate as a result. It "gets us in sync."

What Did Jesus Mean?

Jesus was also popular with little ones. In those days, children were culturally dismissed and powerless. Mark tells us that "they were bringing children to him that he might touch them, and the disciples rebuked them. But when Jesus saw it, he was indignant and said to them, 'Let the children come to me; do not hinder them, for to such belongs the kingdom of God. Truly, I say to you, *whoever does not receive the kingdom of God like a child shall not enter it.*' And he took them in his arms and blessed them" (Mark 10:13–16, italics mine).

When Jesus exhorted His disciples to become like children, do you think it had anything to do with the playful, pure, trusting, dependent, self-forgetful nature of a child?

If I asked you to describe what children are like, what words come to mind? (If playful is not close to the top of your list, I'll be shocked.) Now, reread the italicized portion of the verse above. With arms wide open Jesus receives the children who can offer Him nothing. He blesses them as they are, elevating their ways as a model for us all. Do you think he only meant to bless the serious, linear parts of them?

With the words "*whoever does not receive the kingdom of God like a child shall not enter it,*" He placed His calloused carpenter's hands on our exuberant and playful creative lives and willed our good—releasing us from misdirected constructs of religion, intellect, and power.

Makers, you and I—with our humble lives of play, curiosity, and passion—are blessed by *the* Maker for the benefit of His kingdom glory. It's time we show the world this joyful news on our faces and in our lives.

A Vision of Restoration

In the Old Testament, Zechariah 8 describes the abundance that the Lord wants to restore to His people. Part of His vision includes old men and women chatting in the public squares and the city streets "filled with boys and girls playing there" (verse 5).

Knowing this is God's desire for us reframes heaven in terms of play, fun, and friendship, doesn't it? In other words, you and I can look forward to spending eternity in a place where we will enjoy and play with God forever. Understanding that you and I live in His kingdom *now*, what are we waiting for? It is time we take to the streets!

Looking at play as a spiritual discipline will revitalize even the dustiest old soul. For a joyful life with God and other people, play is key. It fuels creativity, stimulates imagination, generates energy, energizes excitement, provides personal insight, brings laughter, teaches self-control, improves memory, breaks the ice, and bonds us. For makers, play is essential. And there are other benefits as well. For example, play does all these things:

- creates healthy brain connections
- communicates rules
- calms stress and uncertainty
- builds resilience
- develops initiative
- forges resourcefulness
- inspires innovation
- develops social and emotional maturity
- strengthens attachments
- establishes empathy and builds understanding
- forms identity

Play is a feeling we experience as much as any one thing we do. Fun is the point of it—not whether we win or lose. Play takes all forms. We may play games, play with ideas, play sports, play in the great outdoors but, whatever it is to us, play is imperative for the health of our creative soul, the vibrancy of our vocation, and the expansion of God's kingdom.

Connection

Play nourishes our joy. It's obvious. When you and I are delighted to be playing together we incarnate the definition of joy. Doesn't it make sense to prioritize the opportunity to connect with God and one another through play? Our interactions are intended to be en*joy*able. It seems that a reconsideration of our spiritual practices and habits is long overdue. If you're at all like me, you've probably been taking yourself—and your spiritual life—way too seriously. Let's bring it home.

How does God invite you to play?

Perhaps an easier question: What brings you joy?

Curiosity

We all crave novelty. New experiences drive natural curiosity and exploration. These, in turn, point us to play. While novelty gets the ball rolling, the true art of play is found in the relationships and identity we glean as a result.

The Bible instructs us, "But seek first his kingdom and his righteousness, and all these things will be given to you as well" (Matthew 6:33–34 NIV). A curious heart is more open and less judgmental. It seeks God—His heart, wisdom, and ways—not from fear or worry but with playful anticipation of what He will bring each day. The tone of Matthew's text in 7:7 is entirely different when I read with this in mind. Jesus encourages us to ask (and keep on asking), seek (and keep on seeking), and knock (and keep on knocking) from a heart of joyful curiosity—not fear. God's desire is to play and create *with* us.

Beyond the moment of our salvation, you and I can—and should—expect new, novel experiences with God (John 14:12). So stay interested and expectant!

Spiritually and neuroscientifically, we are curious creatures—awarded a big dump of dopamine for every inquisitive effort. Maybe one reason for this is God's foresight: He who knows the end from the beginning most likely recognized that without implanting natural curiosity in our souls, we would not be motivated to search for Him. Like all of us, He longs to be found by those He loves.

Beyond our ultimate search for Him, God also designed our curiosity streak to help us survive and better understand the world and those around us. Fresh out of the womb, infants are rewarded for their inquisitiveness as they first encounter familiar voices and the joyful faces behind them. From there, kids continue to explore by incessantly grabbing, touching, tasting, and asking "Why?" As adults, we are wise to stay curious—like God's toddlers—constantly asking *Why? What is it? Are we there yet?*

Every time we grow and discover things, it is as if a part of us is reborn. Our curiosity is the midwife of creativity—providing the material we draw on to thrive. Born curious, we flourish when our passions and interests are encouraged. We have the superpower to inspire this in one another, often leading to greater creative findings. Cheered on, our inquiring minds look for answers, make discoveries, and establish a sense of agency. In the process, we develop relationships, and as our relational skills develop, so do the bonds between us.

When you or I find ourselves curious about something, we can rest assured that fear is nowhere in our purview. It is a good measure of our joy. What's more, curiosity helps us strengthen relational skills we need at every age. These include:

- collaboration
- negotiation of rules and boundaries
- empathy and understanding
- confidence

Awe and Wonder

God is SO much bigger than we are. When you and I experience His creativity and innovation firsthand, it keeps us wowed and engaged. Not wanting to miss a moment, we are rewarded with a sense of wonder that beckons us to explore, learn, create, and relate more deeply. Each revelation incentivizes our lifelong curiosity and attention. We wonder. We seek. We find. Play reawakens us to the fact that God is delighted to be with us in the most profound, surprisingly simple, and sacred ways.

Recently, *The Harvard Business Review* ran a story entitled "Why You Need to Protect your Sense of Wonder—Especially Now." Addressing resilience after trauma and strain, the authors report that cultivating awe is as important for our well-being as practices centered on gratitude and curiosity. You and I need to put ourselves in the way of awe and wonder!

Contemplating the mind-blowing vastness of our galaxy, the heroism of a good Samaritan, or the beauty of a brush stroke may be all it takes to reset our childlike eyes of wonder.

Marveling about something wonderful we encounter or meditating on the beauty of Scripture effectively refreshes us and reduces anxious thoughts and ruminating fears. It pulls us out of our worry-laden heads and into more benevolent spaces of generosity and compassion.[25]

Wondering where to find some awe? Nature ushers us into opportunities pretty easily.

A group of creative ministry friends I know host a contemplative gathering in the foothills above Denver called "Forest Church." Monthly, they collaborate to create "an interactive outdoor experience with music, reflection, sharing, and hope." Science backs up their outdoorsy method as a means of lowering heart rate, anxiety, stress, and depression.

Too granola for you? Okay, but I encourage you to discover your own "forest" in order to cultivate awe and wonder in your walk with God. Contemplate beauty. Engage with music or art. Savor poetry. Sit under the stars. Marvel at the fact that those stars are still there even in the middle of the day (what Wendell Berry calls "dayblind stars"). All of these moments of awe will leave you closer to God, refreshed, and in a better place.

Consider the practice fodder for your creative mill.

The Lord desires for our childlike wonder to bring us to His studio door in awe. You and I have His heavenly permission to be curious and wonder, to ask (and keep on asking); seek (and keep on seeking); knock (and keep on knocking) in pursuit of His presence and the answers we need for life.

The Sanctified Imagination

You and I get our imagination from God. It is a mighty creative force, so stewarding our imagination well is important. As surely as He speaks to people through His Word, God speaks to us through our imagination—enlightening our spirit, mind, memory, emotions, and understanding. Sometimes, He uses our imagination as a simple invitation to play.

In *The Pursuit of God*, A.W. Tozer wrote that the sanctified imagination "permits us to know that which the senses can never tell us, for by it we are able to see through sense impressions to the reality that lies behind things." The "reality" Tozer describes is God's creative realm. Disciplined for good, our imagination is a huge asset—but probably never more than when we are children looking to play.

Imagination and innovation build on curiosity to empower playful exploration and discovery. As you and I risk stepping out creatively, imagination is the light saber we wield. It provides us with conviction, agency, direction, and—if necessary—protection from the dark side of the Force. In the process, we begin to master some skills and capabilities. Gravitating toward others, we start to find a tribe to call our own. A new sense of belonging fosters connections between us, our mentors, followers, and friends. At some point, we experience disappointment or resistance, encountering social and universal rules that remind us we are not in charge of everything, and in the process, we grow and mature.

In addition, our imagination helps us envision life in someone else's shoes, and thus is at the root of empathy and compassion. And how critical is that? Without empathy and compassion, bad things happen. Bullying runs amuck. Play can turn overly competitive to the point of cheating, bad sportsmanship, or the need to "annihilate" an opponent. And, of course, the absence of empathy and compassion is a hallmark of sociopaths.

Imagination also helps us problem solve and create new things. It seems obvious, but Albert Einstein had a tremendous imagination. Even above knowledge, Albert believed that his imagination was more important to his innovation than anything else. Likewise, our imaginations fuel our creativity and, hence, our play.

Submitted to God and His Word, our imagination is a wide-open playground. Our imagination has no limits, and is a huge asset to our identity, creativity, and play. Ideas, experiences, images, emotions, and senses are creative matchsticks for our imaginations to light on fire. We dream with our eyes open, and when we are imagining new things, the sky's the limit! For example, imagine if the pages of this chapter were electrostatically charged so you could turn each page with a wave of your hand. Magic, right? Nope, just our imagination at play!

Imagining helps us engage whoever or whatever is in front of us. It can also assist us as we seek God. This kind of imagining inspires our transformation. *What If?* is a good question to get the juices of our imagination flowing. So, let's play with it.

- *What if* I were a TED talk speaker, a princess, a competitive mogul skier, a pioneer surviving on the wide-open plains, or (fill in the blank)?
- *What if* my computer was made of chocolate and whenever my writing got really hot (signifying I entered my creative flow), a delicious, perfectly steamed mug of cocoa would pour out of a special port on the side?

Hold on for a minute. Cocoa break.

Ok. I'm back.

- *What if* my making really has an impact? What would life look like five years from now? Who will be alongside me? Where are we? How do I feel? Why does this sound so fun?

How does my future making inspire my life with God and others? What does God think?

Tying our Spirit-led imagination to such questions invites us to do four things: 1) bring ideas to life; 2) reinforce our awareness of our own heart, soul, and mind; 3) invite others into playful possibilities; 4) have fun.

It stirs up energy within and around us when we daydream with God.

In the Great Commandment, when Jesus said to love "with all our mind," the Greek word he chose was *diona*, which literally means "imagination" (Matthew 22:37 NIV). Give yourself permission to set your imagination apart for the Lord's influence on your spiritual life.

Attachment and Attunement

Even in play, it all comes back to who we love most—also known as attachment. Play affirms that our wants and needs matter. In recreational interaction, we are authentically seen, heard, and known. We "feel felt," as interpersonal neurobiologist Dan Siegel explains. This is because play creates limitless opportunities for social-emotional learning and life-giving relationships. Play softens us to one another.

Play fosters a right-brain skill called attunement, which helps us grow into empathetic, compassionate, connected humans. When we "tune in" to one another, we recognize, connect, and engage in an effort to understand. We approach situations as a team and, as a result, we foster understanding, deepen bonds, and expand trust. We get to know and celebrate the best qualities of one another. In addition, when we are attuned to—and delight in—each other, we experience joy. In other words, attunement is the essence of friendship and a step in the direction of healthy identity.

Play not only fosters attunement, it provides health benefits as well. It can lower angst, reduce stress, and help us cope with otherwise unbearable circumstances.

To make our way in the world, play is necessary habit. We must get serious about it!

Flow

A notable aspect in our discussion of play is flow. Not coincidentally, it is also the final element in Catherine Price's definition of fun.

Flow is a state of mind that only happens in the present moment. When you or I enter flow, our prefrontal cortex slows down, allowing us to shift into a more focused, productive state. We may feel super relaxed—as if we are floating. This peaceful state of alpha brainwaves is indicative of the flow zone. If you've ever awakened with a really good idea effortlessly hovering in the background of your morning brain, *that's* what it is like—a chill eureka moment.

Flow simultaneously sharpens our intuition, suspends time, quiets self-consciousness, and supercharges our making. When we are in flow, our dorsolateral prefrontal cortex—where our inner critic lives—shuts down, enabling us to more quickly jump from idea to idea, concept to concept, execution to execution.

Flow greets a creative challenge with norepinephrine and endorphins to keep us going. It masterminds peak performance by allowing our limbic system—the parts of our brain that process memories and emotions—to circumvent slower, more methodical processes of our linear brain. The reward is an additional dump of neurochemicals—dopamine, anandamide, and serotonin—that create sensations of ease, ecstasy, and seemingly effortless skill. Every creative cylinder is firing.

If you think this sounds fun, yep, it is! You've probably been there (in flow, I mean). Whether we know it or not, most of us have—and we want to go back. In fact, play, creativity and flow have this in common—these are feelings we want to experience again and again.

Play and Identity

Beyond being sheer fun, play helps shape who we are and what we know about ourselves. This is our individual identity. God bestows the gift of our authentic, grace-based identity, but play is vital to its unwrapping, and that process requires the participation of others who love us.

On this side of heaven, you and I can only grow our individual identities in the context of our relationships with others and our interaction with God's Word. Enjoyed with friends, play has an almost magical ability to forge the kind of grace-based attachments we need to build a life-giving individual identity—and to help repair what we believe about ourselves when things in our life go wrong.

By ourselves, healthy spiritual, social, physical, emotional, mental development is stunted. So, no Lone Rangers on this faith playground, okay? You and I never outgrow our need for play.

In addition to developing our individual identity, play also informs our group identity.

When I was in grade school, report cards included a box titled "Plays well with others." It was an indicator of social and emotional growth and development. A simple way to strengthen attachment and build group identity—to discover who we consider "our people"—is to play together.

Group identity is made up of those people with whom we connect and identify. Our group identity affords us a sense of belonging, shared values, and beliefs. It also establishes standards of acceptable behavior as we share influence and wisdom in one another's lives. A healthy group identity is essential to the formation of our individual identity.

In fact, by the time we are adults, our group identity becomes more important to us than our individual identity. We may even risk our own well-being in order to protect others in our tribe. Creativity boldly springs from these roots.

Through the years, playfulness continues to define who we are and what we make. Sure, our life can't be all fun and games, but without a healthy balance of work, rest, and play, our sense of inspiration and purpose will drain. Without margin for the sabbath of play, our joy will flatline. Indeed, the pulse of joy can be taken by the amount of play we experience.

Play is a mirror of heaven, dimly lit. Without it, life with God feels dull and eternity fails to capture our imagination. And when this is the case, it is reflected in a lack of creativity with which we approach the Great Commission.

Separating play from our spiritual lives, you and I become Church Lady-like caricatures with a choke-chain on delight. Our image is far from God's. Not an overbearing control freak, our Father *looooooves* when His kids want to play! It's an extravagant gift of love that He gives us. "A shriveled humanity has a shrunken capacity for receiving the rays of God's love," wrote Brennan Manning.[26]

To those outside the Christian faith looking in, there is nothing attractive or transcendent about a playless, emaciated spiritual existence. They don't want that kind of life for themselves—even heaven seems like the last place they would want to spend eternity. And who can blame them!

Whatever your artform, look and listen for the Lord's invitation to play with Him, delight others, and savor what is fun! Meeting God on the playground, our vision suddenly focuses, revealing the fun side of our maker life with God, and a vibrant reality of His enjoyment of us.

MAKER'S AFFIRMATION

Makers cultivate inspiration and sacred imagination by enjoying a fun, full, magnetic life balance.

I am a maker.

Maker Exercises

QUIETING

If you feel like laughing after this, you wouldn't be wrong. Laughter is a great stress reliever, as are shoulder stretches, so here we go:

1. Stand in a comfortable position and take two deep belly breaths. If you have a mirror, use it.
2. On your next inhale, pull your shoulders up toward your ears—as if you are shrugging them. Do this a few times.
3. Continue breathing and shrugging your shoulders, but as you exhale, push the breath out of your lungs with a loud "HA!"
4. Gradually increase the pace until your shrugging and ha's look like you're cracking yourself up for thirty seconds.
5. Wait about thirty seconds. Do two more sets.
6. When finished, consider your overall well-being. How do you feel—emotionally, physically, mentally?

GRATITUDE

Think about the last seven days. Have you had any fun? Add any memories and insights to your Gratitude List. (Hint: going through your calendar can help.) Be sure to capture the experience of all your senses in what you record.

- Out of all the fun you've enjoyed, which has been the most delightful?

- Recreate it in your mind and heart: how did the opportunity come about? Was it spontaneous or planned?
- Who was with you (if anyone)?
- Describe the venue and how you experienced it (with all your senses).
- Where were you?
- What were you doing?
- Why does it stand out in your mind?
- Feel the delight in your body and emotions. Describe what it was like.
- Who do you have to thank for this great time? Share your appreciation accordingly.
- How can you introduce more intentional rhythms of play into your life?

REFLECTION

1. Who or what brings you joy?
2. Do you consider play a spiritual discipline? Why or why not?
3. How does God invite you to play? As you think about this, consider:
    - What makes you laugh?
    - What activities, people or places do you enjoy? Why?
    - Where you experience awe and wonder?
    - What engages your imagination?
    - What do you dream about?
4. When do you experience flow? How do you know when you're in it?
5. How do the people you are close to demonstrate and encourage creativity?
6. How can you encourage more play in your life and relationships?

Visio Divina

FOR CHAPTER 11

John Woods, *Rubber Band Ball* (2021), oil on canvas, Denver, Colorado.

"Truly I tell you, whatever you bind on earth will be bound in heaven, and whatever you loose on earth will be loosed in heaven. Again, truly I tell you that

> if two of you on earth agree about anything they ask for, it will be done for them by my Father in heaven. For where two or three gather in my name, there am I with them."
>
> **MATTHEW 18:18–20 NIV**

READ.

Read the verses slowly and out loud to take in their meaning.

In context, this verse provides a model of proper and prayerful discipline within the Church. Reading this verse recently, something new struck me and it has nothing to do with correction, but with one word. *Bind.* In Aramaic—likely Jesus' language—the word "to bind" literally means "to harness." Whether it be a horse or heavy wind, when we harness something, it is to control its power for a purpose.

REFLECT.

Read the verses again. Note any words or phrases that attract your attention. Does anything deeply resonate as you read? Take time to listen with your heart, soul, and mind. Underline it.

REIMAGINE.

Receive the imagery of *Rubber Band Ball* by artist John Woods as you contemplate the passage. Ask the Lord to enlighten you with holy imagination. Now, read through the scripture again.

- What stands out to you about the painting?
- Is there a sense of energy or stagnancy about it?
- Scripturally speaking, does it draw out anything about the passage you are contemplating?

- Sit still and look closely at the painting's detail. How does it make you feel, physically and emotionally?
- Does the rubber band ball compel you to any particular action? What would it feel like if you took such action? (Imagine it for a minute.)
- As you look at the painting, dwell on the idea of integrating creativity into your spiritual life. Ask God to share His thoughts with you.

CHAPTER 11
ARTFUL INTEGRATION

"We are made to be makers, but as makers we remain lovers. So if you are what you love, then you make what you love. Your cultural labor—whether in finance or fine arts, as a fireman or a first-grade teacher—is animated less by 'principles' that you carry in your head and more by habits of desire that operate under the hood of consciousness."
—JAMES K. A. SMITH, *YOU ARE WHAT YOU LOVE: THE SPIRITUAL POWER OF HABIT*

Integrate. You need to integrate.

The words take me back to the Rocky Mountain retreat time with my friend Jan which I mentioned at the beginning of this book. Even now, they are joyfully bouncing around in me. Deep in my spirit, I heard—and continue to hear—those words. Following nearly a decade of working in the field of Christian spiritual formation, they sank into my soul like a spiritual depth charge—blowing apart all illusions of my discipleship thus far. To be clear, when I heard *integrate*, it didn't strike me in a psychological or neuroscientific way. Instead, I took it as an invitation to bring my whole self to the table—left and right brain, linear and creative.

That invitation set me on a path of discovery that has culminated in the writing of this book. And now I invite you.

By the grace of God, I will always be on the journey to understand the way our hearts, souls, and minds are connected. Want to join me?

When I think about these parts of our being, I'm strikingly aware of something else. God wouldn't call us to live integrated lives if we weren't inclined to slip into the opposite—living disintegrated.

But what does that really look like?

Indeed, there are many ways in which you and I may experience a lack of integration in our creative and spiritual lives. Trauma and sin are two of the clearest examples. Sin separates us from our Creator, making it impossible for us to fully experience the integration of our creativity and spirituality. Trauma—whether from neglect, abuse, loss, experiencing or observing great suffering—can create damage that impairs our ability to experience life as a whole and integrated person.

But other, more subtle things cause us to experience disintegration as well. Let's look at three of them:

Good thinking

An overemphasis on "good thinking" is another way we shut down the creative side of our life with God. Correct thinking and good choices—as effective as they are in some circumstances—do not make us whole. And when we are deceived into believing that they do, we become legalistic (the Pharisees had that down back in Jesus' day, and look where it got them!)

The counterbalance to an overreliance on "good thinking" is embedded within our makeup. If you and I want to find our way back from disintegration, we must rely more heavily on the right brain's relational qualities—qualities that build and nurture secure attachment.

Unwillingness to be known by others

You and I can neither grow nor experience the abundant harvest Scripture talks about if we aren't willing to be deeply known by other people. We limit our growth when we believe that *all* we need is Jesus. (**GASP!**) Yes! We *do* need a relationship with Jesus, but we cannot please God and grow spiritually if we don't go out of our way to know and love other people well. It is in our relationships with others that we work out the kinks of our character. Relationships expose and mature our capacity to love if we let them.

Creating makes our hearts known to us and to those around us. Being known is the most fruitful part of all our making—not to mention our disciple-making. The Bible makes it clear that to "abide in Christ," you and I must focus on fully attaching to Christ and loving one another:

> I am the vine; you are the branches. Whoever abides in me and I in him, he it is that bears much fruit, for apart from me you can do nothing. If anyone does not abide in me he is thrown away like a branch and withers; and the branches are gathered, thrown into the fire, and burned. If you abide in me, and my words abide in you, ask whatever you wish, and it will be done for you. By this my Father is glorified, that you bear much fruit and so prove to be my disciples. . . These things I have spoken to you, that my joy may be in you, and that your joy may be full. "This is my commandment, that you love one another as I have loved you. Greater love has no one than this, that someone lay down his life for his friends.
> John 15:5–7, 12–13 ESV

According to *Strong's Concordance*, the Greek word for *abide* means to stay, remain, rest, or dwell. It sounds like the language of attachment, don't you think? When we abide in Him, our making results in relational fruit-bearing. An unwillingness to be known or to know others hampers the creativity we need for such an assignment. Tending the attachments in our lives is essential to our spiritual growth and creative flow.

Glory stealing

Any making we do carries the potential to bring glory to God, our Maker. If something we create gets noticed, we may be tempted to steal the spotlight—forgetting that the glory belongs to God.

When we steal glory from God, it leaves us further disintegrated.

Stroking our pride by people-pleasing or seeking the affirmation of others is often due to insecure attachment and our lame attempts to prop up our false identity. This disconnects us from our relationship with God. In addition, this kind of disintegration relationally stiff-arms others—keeping them at a distance. They can't get to know the "real" us.

When this happens, it is time to reconsider our motives.

We are not here to build our brand or a creative platform. God is always the only hero of this journey. You and I are here to abide in God's presence and to be a joyful, peaceful, manifest presence to others.

Our being is our true identity rooted in Christ. The branch of our *making* detaches from the vine of *being* in Christ when we seek credit or acclaim. Apart from the vine, we head for the bonfire.

The Westminster Catechism instructs, "the chief end of (man) is to glorify God and enjoy Him forever."

It is about Him. First and always.

Practically speaking, what does it look like for us to glorify and enjoy God? When I co- create with Him, I am changed, and His power shines through! Taking in the reality of God's glory—really experiencing His love and delight in our souls—is to share His creative force.

But apart from Him, you and I can do nothing.

God's glory beams brightest in our lives when we create from wholeness. When you and I create with a sense of connection and wholeness in Him, we thrive.

A Whole-Brain Approach to Creative Living Will Be Relational in Nature

Living a creatively integrated life involves our *whole* brain—our whole life, really. It takes our whole brain to be holy—that means we need to keep both hemispheres flexible. It is important to be mindful of the space that adjustment requires in our spiritual life. Overtraining on left-brain spiritual disciplines without cultivating right-brain issues surrounding relational skills bulks up our spiritual lives in a lopsided way. Both sides of our brain—right hemisphere and left—collaborate to experience fully what it means to be set apart, attuned, and abiding with God in our everyday life.

With the help of God and others, this is where you and I learn to recognize and "metabolize" disintegrating, fear-rooted emotions and behaviors. Unresolved fears lurk around our weaknesses, negative emotions, and bondage to old wounds—reducing our ability to reflect the beams of God's grace. They diminish our emotional capacity, stunt our growth, and keep us stuck.

According to Dr. Jim Wilder, they create the equivalent of a cramp in our brain—specifically in an area vital to our relational and creative capacities, the angular gyrus. Think about it: how creative can we be with a brain cramp?

You and I must leverage our relational design as part of a healthy, lifelong, creative spiritual formation process. Sure, it takes some getting used to, but it is just a matter of reordering things.

In fact, I believe that we benefit when we learn to prioritize the functions of the right side of our brain—those responsible for the relational connection with ourselves, God, and others.

This is not because right-brain functions are more important than left-brain functions, but because relational connections provide both foundation and context for left-brain-leaning procedures like reading Scripture, reading devotionals, praying, and other classic spiritual disciplines. If our right hemisphere is shut down by the disconnection of trauma (big or small), sustainable change—a.k.a. spiritual transformation—won't stick but for a moment.

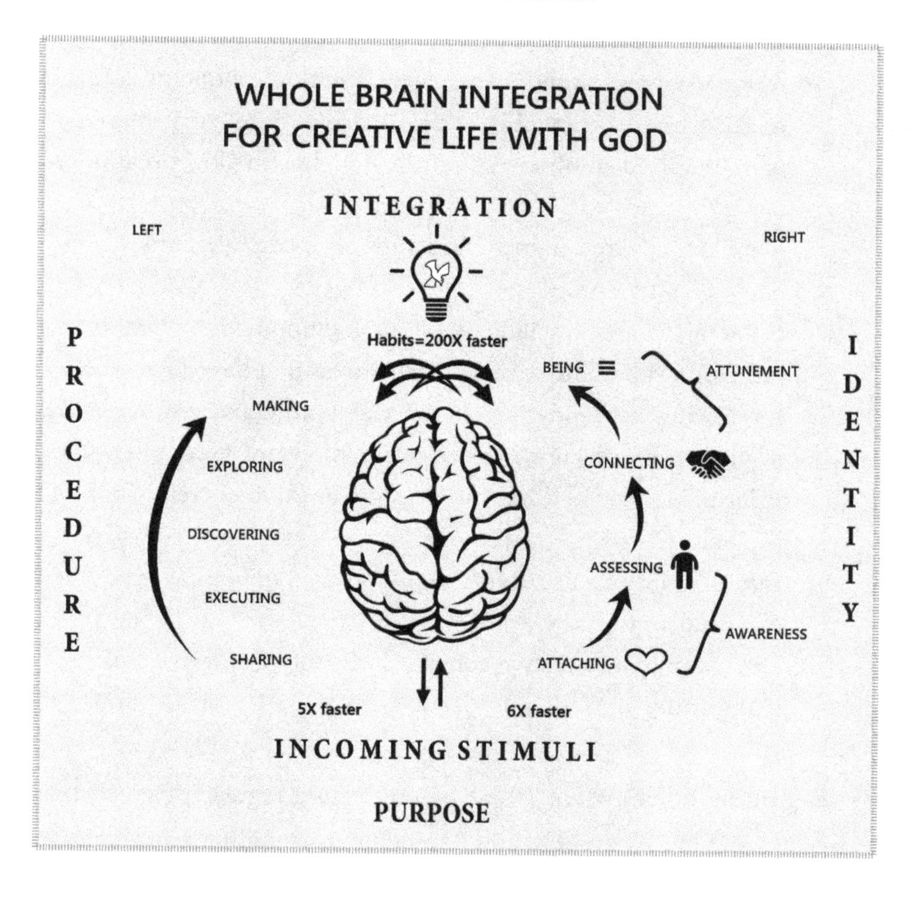

This reprioritization happens as we embrace the practices I've outlined in this book.

Let me summarize them here:

1. Recognizing our attachments and intentionally connecting with who we love most.
2. Remembering gratitude for the gifts of grace we've been given (by God or these special others).
3. Cultivating stillness, settling our central nervous system so we can pay attention to physical, emotional, mental, and spiritual aspects of our heart's lament, body, emotions, thoughts, and relationships.
4. Assessing the specific places where fear or joy has taken up residence in our lamentation, body, emotions, thoughts, and relationships—signaled by the presence or absence of tension, pain, negative emotions, spinning thoughts, shallow breathing, etc.
5. Connecting with others to find and share empathy and compassionate support.
6. Remembering and telling our story. Examining helpful and unhelpful experiences and the narratives that have formed us.
7. Identifying our God-given individual, family, and group identity in the process of knowing and being known by God and others.
8. Prioritizing play and relaxation necessary to fuel creativity and shalom.
9. Listening for our heart's song—"God themes"—that strengthen our creative purpose.
10. Discovering our creative commission—the purpose of our making.

Beginning our time with God by cultivating regular practices that build Attachment, Awareness, and Attunement strengthens our identity.

These skills help "disciple" us from the base of our brainstem in an upward and counterclockwise direction—intentionally prioritizing the right-hemispheric functions. Specifically, we are establishing habits that hone our neuropathways to help us better quiet, be present, regulate emotions, connect with God and others, define values, and create character—all of which contribute to the establishment of a secure identity.

The identity center of our brain is located just behind our right eye, in the right orbital prefrontal cortex. This region is also home to our "executive center," where we make decisions that impact every area of our life. The healthier, more joyful, and more secure our identity, the better our ability to make good, neurologically balanced decisions. In contrast, when we are relationally shut down, all we have to draw on is left-brain logic.

I don't mean to imply things are cut and dry on this neurological trip. I merely suggest that our educational and religious systems train most of us to *do* spiritual life in left-brained, logical ways. We are taught how to efficiently plow through projects and goals as we uphold the appearance and behaviors good Christian people *should*. The problem with approaching things this way is that it loads our spiritual life with left-brain assignments—cutting off our capacity to abide with God and others. To the left brain, relationships are an afterthought if not an obstacle to spiritual "productivity." This behavior cements our individualistic, Western-thinking, "get-'er-done" tendencies. The practical "hows" and "whys" of relationship get overlooked.

On this score, I have a confession: when I was younger, I had a lot of strong opinions about youth groups that seemed more like play groups. In my judgy, religious head, I thought the skits, relays, games, and hangout time were childish—a waste of time. This stuff was more milk than meat for anyone *really* after God, I told myself. I didn't perceive the importance of the bonds formed through the enjoyment of one another, play, exercise, and laughter *before* diving into teaching about God's Word.

Distancing myself from the discomfort of being found relationally clumsy, I fortified the walls around my weaknesses and failures with biblical facts, Scripture, and thinking about God. Because this was the emphasis within my religious community *and* I had experienced wounds in different relationships, these self-protective ideas fit my theology well. Why would I question them? I didn't realize the negative implications on my spiritual and creative life. In the big picture, my heady approach blocked the flow of both.

There is no use fighting it: it is just how our brains are made.

Research regarding the state of Christian discipleship at large supports that we've been approaching our spiritual life backward. As a result, you and I live dis-integrated spiritual lives. We cannot flourish spiritually, relationally, emotionally, mentally, physically, or creatively if we don't integrate our whole selves.

For those of us who have gone down this path on our spiritual journey, all we need to do is turn around, head back, and take a right—to "the road less traveled," a relational way of spiritual life with God and others.

The Great Commission builds on relationships, not data. Discipleship *is a* relationship, and, as part of our spiritual practice, our making *is* relational. Both are defined and refined in our relationship with God, self, and others. These permeate every aspect of our identity and influence the character of what we are creating. Our making and its subjective meaning leave a mark. We discover and express more of our true and creative selves.

In reality, we cross back and forth between right- and left-brain functions via the corpus callosum. Think of it as a bridge that connects the neural energies of each hemisphere to "cross over," as needed. Everything changes when those energies are guided across the bridge in right- brain, relational ways—our life with God and others becomes more interactive. Training in joyful practices, you and I settle in from our quieted, aware, grateful, and connected selves *before* we cross to take action in procedural, left-brain ways.

By learning to value and keep relationships more important than any project or problem that arises, we break old chains of expectation, comparison, and fear—freeing us to act from a joyful, Spirit-led identity. When we lead with our creative side, the Spirit-empowered, transcendent work we create becomes an extension of who we love and all we are. Our maker lives become an interplay of healthy identity, logical processes, and the creative glory of God. Spirit-led inklings turn into works of art laden with ever unfolding meaning and impact. Our maker life and discipleship journey flow and flourish.

This kind of making joyfully expresses our whole, integrated being.

In *The Soul of Desire,* Dr. Curt Thompson writes, "For us to become complete—to complete God's work of our being made in his image—we must enter into this most grounded facet of who God is: an artist who makes because he first loves what he is about to create."[27] So it should be with us: we are makers creating because we first love God. And we love better—create from loving relationship—as a result (1 John 4:18–20). What a joyful prospect!

MAKER'S AFFIRMATION

Makers holistically glorify God, drawing others to Him through their authentic way of being.

I am a maker.

Maker Exercises

QUIETING

Read through the following instructions before you begin.

- Put on some instrumental music.
- Lie down on the floor or sit in a chair with your feet comfortably on the floor.
- Turn your palms up in a posture of surrender and willingness to receive.
- Begin by taking a few slow, deep breaths.
- As you breathe in, pray: *God, I want to know you.*
- As you breathe out, pray: *God, I want to be known by you.*
- Repeat this several times until you sense a release.
- Sit in stillness for a moment before opening your eyes.

GRATITUDE

Remember a time you felt deeply peaceful. Feel it in your body. What was it like for you? What were the circumstances? Was it a time with God or another person, or were you alone? Add this memory to your Gratitude List. Detail it, recounting the whole experience with your senses and emotions.

REFLECTION

1. On a scale of 1 (not at all) to 5 (very), how creatively integrated is your spiritual life? Explain.
2. This chapter reviewed ten practices to build Attachment, Awareness, and Attunement to establish connection, healthy community, and strengthen our identity—our *be*ing. Which of these are already habits of yours? Are there any that you need to cultivate in your life?
3. Does taking unhurried time to notice your emotional and physical state come easily to you in your time with God?
4. Would you describe your conversation with God as interactive and ongoing? Explain.
5. Ask God what He wants you to know about this chapter. Journal your impressions for five minutes.
6. Is your creative life feel well integrated into your spiritual life or disintegrated? How does it feel in your body? What emotions does this stir up?
7. Do you relate to the areas of disintegration addressed in this chapter (sin, trauma, good thinking, unwillingness to be known, glory stealing)?
8. Before you begin, ask the Lord to share His insights with you. Read 1 John 4:15–21 three times slowly—circling any words or phrases that jump out at you as you do. What do these verses tell you about living an integrated life with God and others?

MAKER PROMPT

Make something that reminds you to shine for God and the sake of others.

Visio Divina

FOR CHAPTER 12

Janet Brooks-Gerloff, *On the Road to Emmaus* (1992), oil on canvas, Kornelimunster Abbey, Aachen, Germany. (Copyright 2023 Artists Rights Society (ARS), New York / VG Bild-Kunst, Bonn. Used by permission.)

READ.

Take your time reading the Scripture below aloud.

> And behold, on that very day two of them were going to a village named Emmaus, which was sixty stadia from Jerusalem. And they were talking with each other about all these things which had taken place. While they were talking and discussing, Jesus

Himself approached and *began* traveling with them. But their eyes were kept from recognizing Him. And He said to them, "What are these words that you are exchanging with one another as you are walking?" And they came to a stop, looking sad. One *of them*, named Cleopas, answered and said to Him, "Are You *possibly* the only one living near Jerusalem who does not know about the things that happened here in these days?" And He said to them, "What sort of things?" And they said to Him, "Those about Jesus the Nazarene, who proved to be a prophet mighty in deed and word in the sight of God and all the people, and how the chief priests and our rulers handed Him over to be sentenced to death, and crucified Him. But we were hoping that it was He who was going to redeem Israel. Indeed, besides all this, it is *now* the third day since these things happened. But also some women among us left us bewildered. When they were at the tomb early in the morning, and did not find His body, they came, saying that they had also seen a vision of angels who said that He was alive. And *so* some of those who were with us went to the tomb, and found it just exactly as the women also had said; but Him they did not see." And *then* He said to them, "You foolish men and slow of heart to believe in all that the prophets have spoken! Was it not necessary for the Christ to suffer these things and to come into His glory?" Then beginning with Moses and with all the Prophets, He explained to them the things *written* about Himself in all the Scriptures. And they approached the village where they were going, and He gave the impression that He was going farther. And *so* they strongly urged Him, saying, "Stay with us, for it is *getting* toward evening, and the day is now nearly over." So He went in to stay with them. And it came about, when He had reclined *at the table* with them, that He took the bread and blessed *it*, and He broke *it* and *began* giving *it* to them. And *then* their eyes were opened and they recognized Him; and He vanished from their sight. They said to one another, "Were our hearts not burning within us when He was speaking to us on the road, while He was explaining the Scriptures to us? And they got up that very hour and returned to Jerusalem, and found the eleven gathered together and those who were with them, saying, "The Lord has really risen and has appeared to Simon!" They began to relate their experiences on the road, and how He was recognized by them at the breaking of the bread."

LUKE 24:13–35 NASB

REFLECT.

Read the verses again, underline anything that stands out to you.

- What do you notice as you engage these words today? Patiently, quiet yourself to listen with your whole body and soul. What is the Holy Spirit showing you?

REIMAGINE.

Direct your attention to *On the Road to Emmaus* by Janet Brooks-Gerloff as you continue to reflect on the passage. Ask the Lord to guide you in the following steps:

- Consider its composition and color, the postures and landscape.
- Where is your eye drawn?
- What story does it tell you? Make note of what you notice as you continue to survey the scene.
- Who do you identify with or where do you imagine yourself in the painting? Explain.
- Does it echo the words or phrases that stood out to you in the reading?

RESPOND.

- Prayerfully respond to the Lord about your interaction with His Word and the painting.
- What is God's invitation to you? Are you compelled to take action or sit with Him about what He's revealed to your heart?
- Quietly contemplate what you've received. Thank God for His faithfulness to meet you here.

CHAPTER 12

CREATIVE COMMISSION

"God is the map whereby we locate the setting of our life. That God is the water in which we launch our life raft. That God is the real thing from which and toward which we receive our being and identify ourselves. It follows that the kind of God at work in your life will determine the shape and quality and risk at the center of your existence. It matters who God is."
– WALTER BRUEGGEMAN

History catalogs artists who were commissioned to paint, sculpt, or otherwise make their original works to flaunt a leader's power and authority. For instance, during the Renaissance, Michelangelo was reportedly forced by Pope Sixtus IV to accept the commission for the Sistine Chapel ceiling. Despite the impressive commission (estimated to be worth $2.9 million in today's dollars), Michelangelo resisted the opportunity because he considered himself a sculptor—*not a painter*. Despite his protests, the artist was required to honor the ego of a pompous Pope.

We've all seen the end result, and it's one of the world's most celebrated works of art—one that relays the Bible narrative for those fortunate to see it.

But the process was not without pain and drama. He spent four years, every day, flat on his scaffolding-supported back for something he did not feel called or equipped to do. Every. Day. Also, Michelangelo's theology did not align with that of the Catholic Church, so much so that by the time he finished painting the chapel (ceiling *and* altar), the Vatican suspended his pension and threw in the insult of painting over some portions of his work.

Have you ever had to muster your motivation for a mission that wasn't yours? I can't recommend it. Labeled "a creative" often leads to things like a VBS draft notice or church event to-do's (*She'll do it—she's so creative at wordsmithing/event planning/painting/staging/name your gifting)*. Listen, initially we are all flattered when that happens, but we must be careful to discern if we want to get on the same train before we jump aboard.

Whether it is the result of misdirected zeal or a misconstrued sense of obligation, you and I are each uniquely called to the Great Commission by God alone. This calling is the result of our relationship with Him and uniquely inherent to our identity. No one else gets to recruit us for their own show or dictate what our calling may be. We are not a tool in anyone's hand but God's.

When we are shoehorned into making that isn't ours, it is upsetting. From experience, it elicits dread in me. Whenever you and I are afraid, angry, sad, hopeless, ashamed, or disgusted, our light dims. Feeling all alone and unseen at such times creates the ultimate existential crisis, and nobody needs that! So why do we hide and harbor those feelings?

Especially for makers, Christian culture isn't always clear on that point. Just because I *can* make creative things, your need for them doesn't get to commandeer my creative skillset unless God is on board.

That just leads to burnout.

A maker's personal version of the Great Commission will always engage and focus our creative energy, heart first—authorized and empowered by the Holy Spirit. We are to steward that energy—lending our effort to *what He directs*. This is an invitation to join God where He is at work. Acting out of our Great creative Commission, the kingdom comes to earth for all to see—in and through us. What lights us up representing the light of Christ to a dark world! Plugging into the empowerment of the Holy Spirit makes it hard for people to miss.

The restoration and affirmation of Jesus brightens our capacity to make. At the heart of it, that is because our creativity is a matter of dependency—our abiding attachment to God, not somebody else's agenda.

With that being said, let's talk about what God is calling you to do, be, and create. For greater insight into what your creative commission might be—and what might be standing in the way of living that commission with greater impact and passion—ask yourself these three questions:

1. "Am I hiding or shining?"

You and I are lights in a dark world. We are meant to shine and show the world the blessings of life with God.

Consider Jesus' words:

> "Here's another way to put it: You're here to be light, bringing out the God-colors in the world. God is not a secret to be kept. We're going public with this, as public as a city on a hill. If I make you lightbearers, you don't think I'm going to hide you under a bucket, do you? I'm putting you on a light stand. Now that I've put you there on a hilltop, on a light stand—shine! Keep open house; be generous with your lives. By opening up to others, you'll prompt people to open up with God, this generous Father in heaven."
>
> **MATTHEW 5:14–16 MSG**

Thanks to advances in neuroscience, we now know that when we live a creative, integrated life, we can shine brighter than ever. And what lights us up draws others!

The idea of embracing a better way to shine reminds me of when we began to make the transition from incandescent bulbs to LED. I'll be honest, I didn't want to make the switch—especially at first, when all LEDs promised was a harsh blue-white light. But now—thanks to improvements in technology—LEDs offer warm light, energy savings, and they're less expensive. In other words, they're better all around.

You and I are lightbulbs. We are meant to shine and show the world the blessings of a creative and warmly connected life with God.

If you've been relying most on the left side of your brain to serve God and others, the learning curve to embrace your right-brain creativity may not be comfortable at first, but it's a transition worth making.

Don't hide your light. Let it shine!

2. "Am I filled with fear or fire?"

A thoughtful combination of theology, spiritual formation, and neuroscience provided me with new insights into another familiar passage of Scripture, Luke 24:13–33.

Luke describes how two disciples were walking on the road to Emmaus shortly after the death of Jesus. As they walked, they talked about the traumatic events the disciples had recently witnessed. After the brutal and shocking death of their mentor and friend, I can imagine that their emotions were all over the map. They undoubtedly felt anger and disgust at the injustices exacted by their government and religious leaders, grief over the loss of their savior friend, shame that they had been helpless to do anything to stop the crucifixion, despair over the outcome, and deeply troubled by fear of what may befall them as Jesus' followers.

Neurologically, the disciples were probably hunkered down in the back of their brain as they rehashed the traumatic events to which they had just been exposed. Mentally, the two were far away from the relational frontlines of faith and their individual callings. While being together under such circumstances was better than being alone, it was not enough to help them out of the state of fear they were in. The "big six" of fear-based emotions was flooding their fight-or-flight system just about the time a stranger met them on the road.

Joining the disciples on their journey, the stranger listened to their stories, grief, and fears, and responded by reminding them of relevant scriptures and prophecies about the Messiah. The three continued along the road, talking for quite a while before the disciples got to their destination and invited Him to stay for dinner. Not until the mystery traveler broke the bread did they recognize their companion was Jesus! *Fear* had blinded them up to that time, but all at once love healed their vision and warmed the reflection of their hearts.

> They said to each other, "Were not our hearts burning within us as he was speaking with us on the road and explaining the Scriptures to us?"
> **LUKE 24:32 NASB**

For many of us, fear blinds us to the creative potential of our calling and commission. But consider the cost. When we focus on our fears, we miss out on so much—starting with recognizing the very presence of God in our midst!

Are we choosing fear over joy? Are we unaware of God with us as a result?

An encounter with Jesus reminded the Emmaus disciples of their individual identities as well as His final Commission. No doubt, it lit a fire in both of them. I imagine the two running the whole seven miles back to Jerusalem in order to encourage the others and tell everyone that it was time to take the discipleship show on the road!

If you have been filled with fear, it's not too late to let Jesus replace that fear with a new fire in your soul!

Didn't we feel our hearts burn within us while he talked to us on the road and opened the Scriptures to us?

The experience of the disciples can be ours as well. Ask God to remove your fear and ignite passion and fire in your heart for all that He is calling you to do, be, and create. Then, begin today living your life in faith and anticipation. Expect that He will meet you on the road, because He will! He is, after all, Immanuel—God with us. Our Hero is also always with us. He will remake our making, redirect our direction, rearrange our song.

3. "Am I marching to someone else's drum or singing the heart song God gave me?"

How do we begin seeking God's input into our creative commissions? Among other things, we can engage in prayerful imagining, we can ask God for discernment, and we can seek out wise counselors and mentors. In doing so, we can discover not only creative direction, but also relational connection.

And if we dare to calm our souls and learn to listen, there's something else we can discover: our heart song.

Many of us have never listened to our heart's unique song. To do so takes us full circle, back to quiet places in which we can experience the blending of harmonies made up of our longings and laments, gratitude and joy, gifts and skills. Its melody weaves its way throughout our life story.

To discover our heart song, we must learn to listen. We must learn to listen to our souls and bodies where refrains of the melody can be found.

Most importantly, we must learn our song from the Master Composer Himself.

Sadly, especially in our churches, many don't think God speaks to them—let alone co-creates a song in their heart. Yet, in big and small ways, usually quite creatively, He speaks all the time! There is a sacred weight and a feeling to His words.

Sometimes I recognize His voice by a responsive stirring in my own spirit. Sometimes, it is by the way his message to me aligns with His Word and character. Other times, a quickening warmth sparks a flame in my heart and I know: *God is speaking. Pay attention to this! Here is some creative kindling. Share it! Set the world on fire with this revelation. Fan the flame of my holy making!*

I have a habit. Most days, I begin with quiet, untethered silence and nothing available to lead my mind off on one of its many trails. Before I read my Bible, I ask the Lord how He wants to spend time with me and then I listen. Whatever I hear is reflectively recorded, sketched, or painted in my soft, green leather-bound journal. Some days, I simply bask quietly in God's presence—not a word makes the page. But more often than not, I see something, hear a word, or sense something that speaks truth to me about who God is, who I am, or where the Lord is in different circumstances. Whatever is quickened, I will study where He leads me in Scripture.

A few months ago, my morning began a little differently. I was spending time listening quietly for direction from the Lord when my phone rang. It was Theressa, a dear friend of mine. She told me she was struggling—feeling dry, lost, wandering—and wondering where God was. She was weary. Why wasn't he showing up? She was sick of it. . . and lonely.

As her words spilled out, I listened, unhurried, all the while lifting her in prayerful thoughts to my Father.

As the details tumbled out with her tears, an image began to form in my mind. I saw my friend standing on a canvas of barren land—a discouraged soul wandering away from a freshwater stream snaking across the landscape, while tempestuous clouds rained down all around. Her back was to the lighter side of the storm, meaning she had determined to march into the worst of the desolate desert squall.

The image was too vivid not to try and capture. When I hung up the phone, I loaded the oil paints on my palette and reached for a knife. *What brush to begin? Ahh, a palette knife!*

I don't often use a palette knife for an entire painting—but boy, is it fun, adding texture as the paint globs and spreads and swipes colors across a canvas. For me, in this piece, it became the perfect tool to reflect and release my friend's chaotic and bound emotion. As the knife edged the surface, I thought about Theressa, what she had shared, asked the Lord how He wanted to meet her. I prayed. *Please, would you speak, Lord?*

I stood back and waited for his response. We interacted, God and me.

Quiet.

Listening.

Then I knew.

More weeping.

The clouds needed to be heavier with burden, more volatile with weeping sheets of rain.

Moments later, I rested my pallet knife on the easel. Something was still missing, I could sense it. But notorious for overworking a painting, I stepped away. I snapped a picture on my phone to send to Theressa before going upstairs.

I hadn't been upstairs long when the Lord pointed out the element I had overlooked: the tiny journeyman figure—my friend—needed a halo. She was a saint, needing to do what saints sometimes had to do.

So, with the tiniest flick of gold on the knife, "St. Theressa" had a glistening halo. Just then, it struck me: that much light over her and on her back would have to cast a shadow. That would mean the shadow would go before her. *Not sure I like the idea, but it is where it needs to be.*

I continued to meditate on the small smudge at the figure's feet and, slowly, it was like a revelation: The smudge was the shadow of God's glory. *Wow! Thank you, Father. Thank you for your guidance into and through the desert. I bless your name and thank you for your provision in the water and the storm. And, God, thanks for the reminder that you go before your saints. We walk in the shadow of Your glory. Amen.*

That day, something was kindled—a new creative medium of prayer.

Actually, from the moment the image appeared in my head to its seemingly effortless completion, it felt like an out-of-body experience. I was drawn into the process, curious, without agenda, exploring, discovering, imagining, in awe, with God, with my friend. Time stood still, vim flowed. The painting had God's brushstrokes all over it. As a result of what we shared I felt closer to Theressa and Him.

My art had been transformed into an energized, cathartic intercession on my friend's behalf. The three of us connected in its creation: God, Theressa, and me. The flash of concept in my imagination became a painting of a prayer, listening, and praise. Deeper than my words could address, as the paint took to the canvas it told me a story. Before paint could dry, the shared creative experience with God had created a deeper soul connection with Him and with Theressa as well.

With Theressa's tender, teary smile looking back at me over a Zoom screen, I showed her the work and interpreted what the three of us had made. And in the process, the art of God's playfulness, connection, and flow released creative healing for Theressa and for me as well.

This time, my heart's song was played on a canvas.

Your Creative Commission Is Part of the Great Commission

God has invited us all to take part in the Great Commission, drawing other disciples into relationship with Him. I believe he goes further, designing for each of us a unique great *creative* commission—a purposeful place where we can sing our heart songs in ways that draw other disciples into creative relationship with Him. It is a co-mission, really, because we are never alone in it.

When you and I discover our great creative commission, the dimensions of our whole self shimmers—like a crescendo of our heart's song. Our making is the creative mission that holds the song of our hearts. Frederick Buechner famously penned, it is "the place where your deep gladness and the world's deep hunger meet." He defines "deep gladness" as the call of one's true, enduring and authentic self that produces deep joy.

If you are wondering what *your* great creative commission is, start by looking around.

- What steadily grieves your heart?
- What creates deep gladness in your soul?
- Where is there a specific invitation to offer your heart song?
- Are you hearing God's invitation to join Him or just a need someone has expressed? When an opportunity to make something that matters stokes a fire in your soul, the most important thing is to discern whether this mission is something God is inviting you into. If emotions, outside influences, or personal need cloud your ability to hear from Him, seek out others to pray about the opportunity with you. He leads us with shalom—a perfect balance of joy and peace.

It has taken me many years, but I now realize that that the form and weight of these opportunities is not mine to bear, but His. My making is not about the end product, but about the connection I experience with God and with others. *Where does God want me? What is He trying to creatively say? Who does He want to reach? How does He want me to make it known?*

Breaking the bread of this communion with Him, our times of connection resonate with deep warmth and abiding shalom. My eyes are opened, my heart aflame. Maybe that is why I readily return to Luke 24:32 so often: "Were not our hearts burning within us while He was speaking with us on the road, while He was explaining the Scriptures to us?" I am on the Emmaus Road.

Making cracks open my soul—integrating my emotions, thoughts, and skills and ushering in divine revelation in the process. And as the process of making lights me up, I not only see and know—I also experience being seen and being known. God's light shines through my making!

Just when my left-brain thinks it has things in hand, my right has ways of opening up new depths of mystery. I just have to be patient—wholly attentive, aware, and attuned.

Keep an eye out for ways you can enjoy God as you go about your making. People notice your delight, they may discover a side of God they might never otherwise seen—their souls crack open a little, too. A light comes on, allowing them to understand something they might never have otherwise grasped.

Just as Jesus's parables revealed timeless truths in the fabric of creative storytelling, God-insights and reflections are woven into the fabric of our creativity. Our making brings light to people, and that light brings glory to God, you know?

Embracing Immanuel's presence in the creative process assures us that what we are creating is extraordinary—an intimate wonder whether anyone ever sees our work or not. In that, we are all at once vulnerable and secure. Hand in hand with God, our trust, secure identity, and creativity grow.

You and I are able to do our best work *with God.*

As we commune with God, we interactively co-create from bonds of deep attachment, awareness, attuned connection, and secure identity—a place of intimacy. This, in turn, creates neuropathway-worn habits reflective of *hsed* (grace-based, unconditional, loving, covenantal) community—white-matter evidence of His active work in our spiritual maturity.

Our making lights us up as it brings light to the world—and the world is drawn to the twinkle of joy in our eyes.

When God leads us to share our making, this is what we are doing: sharing His heart. It is not up to us, so let's not be timid or stingy with our creation. It isn't weird, it is obedience. We should expect that there are others whose hearts will also be broken open by what we offer. Watch for it! Undone people affirm the evidence of God's glory that inhabits the special gift we are to the community—not as a product to be used but as a person for whom the Lord has marvelous plans.

These fellow creatives are the ones who watch and wait with us. They champion us as we grow and remind us to let grace make us brave as we create. And we must do the same for them—bravely and authentically. Let's call out the good, true, and beautiful making God is working within one another.

We are makers in what has been a thinkers' world, up to this point. But now it is out in the open.

Artful apprentices of logic—and all those previously seated at the children's table—at last gain the floor.

Indeed, the truth is that we need thinking makers *and* making thinkers in the world—intentional people stewarding their creativity, united and delighted to be together as we champion His kingdom. Together, makers and thinkers release a generative force of God's creative mission in the world. To that end, celebrating one another is an essential part of God's vision for us and our purpose within His kingdom.

In *The Divine Conspiracy,* Dallas Willard wrote, "We were built to count, as water is made to run downhill. We are placed in a specific context to count in ways no one else does. That is our destiny." As makers, we have more to offer the body of Christ than most of us have imagined.

So, no more excuses for hiding your light. The joyful light of Christ burns most brightly when the mission of our making is the match that we purposefully strike. It not only warms our hearts but offers light and warmth to others who, upon drawing near, will be changed forever by the light of His joy in our eyes.

MAKER'S AFFIRMATION

Makers hold their redemptive purpose humbly before God, themselves, and others—inviting collaboration for a kingdom cause.

I am a maker.

For more help defining your heart's song, see the Appendix.

Maker Exercises

Integrating Immanuel Creativity

Throughout *Makers in a Thinkers' World,* we've introduced various practices to help us cultivate the peace and joy necessary for healthy emotional, physical, and spiritual growth. Whatever your spiritual rhythms, I hope you clearly take away the significance of beginning time with God and others by creating space for quieting and gratitude. When we do, this commitment helps us show up as our whole selves.

The Creative Interaction with Immanuel Worksheet invites our souls to integrate—our whole heart, soul, and mind come before God and a sacred few. The exercise guides the various Maker Exercise skills we've learned in a single, relational flow with God. Unlike emptying mindfulness practices, Immanuel Interactions begin as we quiet ourselves and acknowledging the goodness of the One who gives and continues to be with us as we process our emotions and sensations—good and bad. Knowing we are seen, safe, soothed, and secure in our attachment with God and others changes us. This simple process demonstrates how to recognize life's pain and trauma in our mind, body, and relationships so we can metabolize it out of our system and return to joy.

Through it all, God's indwelling joy and peace companion our every step. This connection to Him is essential to our growth and maturity. Attachments rupture when you or I encounter stresses that steal our joy and peace (a.k.a. fear-based emotions) and leave us feeling all alone—interpersonally and spiritually. Relational ruptures shut us down.

Engaging and interacting with God helps us repair what is ruptured, return to joy, and reconnect with God and others. The Creative Interaction with Immanuel Worksheet is a great tool to reconnect with God, ourselves, and those around us.

Up until now, we have explored topics and practices in a specific, neurological order. **Quiet. Gratitude. Awareness. Attunement. Identity.** This specific order restores our brain's relational capacity. Our mind and body require relationships to help us move through distress. Each time we blow a relational fuse, we start the repairs at the base of the brain—where our core attachments live. From there, we learn to release the upset of trauma as we make our way up the emotional, physical, and spiritual labyrinth of brain circuitry to the prefrontal cortex—where our healthy identity lives. By doing so, we reconnect the relational fuses blown by fear. Following this order, our brains are able to process fear-bred problems and make purposeful steps back to our true selves.

Once back "online," you and I can engage in the delight of being together described as joy. And crops of creativity sprout here!

Here is a way to connect with Immanuel—God *with us*—through it all. As always, we begin with quiet and gratitude. Then, we search for our capacity to connect with His still small voice.

My prayer is that this tool helps you find your place at His banquet table of joy alongside other makers and thinkers. I'll be looking for you!

Makers Exercise

Creative Interaction with Immanuel Worksheet

Putting it all together

Established fact: bushes are known to combust in the sweltering desert heat spontaneously (we talked about it in Chapter 1).

When the bush burst into flame, Moses hadn't yet "arrived" as God's leader. After murdering an Egyptian slave driver, Moses fled from Pharoah's palace to his would-be father-in-law's goat farm. When Moses encountered God in the burning bush, he was tending goats. By "tending," I mean that he made sure they were nourished, guided, and protected. Because shepherds were culturally considered among the lowest of the low, the former prince of Egypt must have had a meek, humble nature and performed as a decent enough shepherd.

The question remains: what about *this* bush caused *this* shepherd to turn his attention to the side and encounter God? Maybe he noticed a feeling or a heavy sense of God's holy presence? Whatever caused Moses to pay attention, his action—turning, looking, and listening—drew him closer.

And among all the other shepherds out there, why did God appear to Moses in the burning bush? What made Him choose Moses to lead the Israelites through the Wilderness? Could it be that through His eyes of grace, the Lord saw Moses's attentive, obedient heart could handle the weight of His authority before His people?

Whatever the case, God and Moses had cultivated a life of secure attachment, self-awareness, attunement with others, and a solid sense of with-God identity—the kind of character that the Lord knew He could use to set people free. Even though Moses was not perfect, he was a relationally bonded servant of God. Who you love most affects what you become, you know.

I tell you this partly because the following exercise reflects Exodus 3. Southern California marriage and family therapist Sungshim Loppnow first noted the scriptural connection to Immanuel Journaling. It is a practice designed to direct you through well-ordered steps of quieting, gratitude, awareness, and attunement and guide you back to a joyful connection with your true identity, God, and others who love you. Not coincidentally, the discipline vertically integrates us as we move through it—from the base of our brainstem to the top of our right prefrontal cortex.

In this adaptation, feel free to incorporate words, images, sensations, and emotions in any medium—traditional journaling style or another "art" form. Create each response however you want—it doesn't have to be in written form. Go with your flow. The only limit is time. Please take four minutes for steps 1–7—or as expert Kitty Wilder used to say, "Think of it as texting with God." The most important thing is to use the time for connection and interaction with God.

At any time during the process, if you lose your peace, feel pressured, anxious, fearful, or begin to get upset, simply return to your original gratitude memory. When you find peace again, continue the worksheet. For step 1, you will respond from your perspective. Write from God's perspective on steps 2–7.

When we joyfully make and share story and meaning, it becomes embedded as part of who we are. The following is an adaptation of

"Immanuel Journaling." Whether going through this book alone or with a group, I encourage you not to skip steps 8 and 9.

I encourage you to practice quieting and keeping a list of gratitude memories to draw on as you weekly or monthly revisit this exercise. In between Immanuel exercises, my friend Annette told me she keeps a plastic bag with pictures, treasures she's found, mementos of gratitude experiences, along with a notebook of her Gratitude List, prayers, sermon notes, etc. When she sits down to complete the exercise, she easily refreshes her memory by looking over what she's gathered and written in the time between, asking the Holy Spirit to guide her. Using a highlighter, she calls out what God calls her attention to in the moment. It is a rich point of reconnecting.

This brings up the most important aspect of creative interaction with Immanuel: more than a perfect creative product or healing, relationally *connecting* with God is our goal. He is with you always.

(Note: This is a longer exercise than other chapters. Please calendar a "Maker Date" for this exercise—a free afternoon for you and God to connect and create together.)

1. **Quieting.**
   Light a candle to remind you of God's presence and warmth. Then, put on some soft, instrumental (wordless) music for the exercise. As you do, relax your body, close your eyes, and take deep, full breaths. Spend two to three minutes becoming still and centered on God's presence.
2. **Gratitude**
   Dear God, I'm thankful for. . .
   My dear child, ______________________ (write God's response to your gratitude)

3. **I see you.** (Write what you believe God sees, what you think he observes in you, including your physical sensations.) Each step offers examples to help you start processing your real-time emotions and sensations. At this moment, you may be in a good place or aware of a pain or problem you have.

   Appreciation-building example:

   I see you on your porch, remembering how you enjoyed yourself yesterday. I see you then as well. You were warm, relaxed, and so caught up in the gift I gave you. You felt My breeze touch your face. A little smile is on your lips, and you are stretching out as you recall every detail. You particularly enjoyed . . .

   Problem-resolution example:

   I see you. . . breathing anxiously, and your shoulders are so tight and uncomfortable. Your heart is heavy, and your eyes are downcast—I see them filling with tears.

4. **I hear you. . .** (Write what you believe God hears you saying to yourself.)

   Appreciation-building example:

   I hear you. . . wish your children could have enjoyed this with you. You wonder why you don't take time for this more often and then suddenly wonder if you have thanked me. You wonder if there are other places in your life where you miss the chance to express your appreciation. I know the idea bothers you, but I am not distracted by it. I see you return to your gratitude memory—feeling close to me and grateful again.

   Problem-resolution example:

   I hear you saying, "How did I ever let this happen? How can I get out of this mess?" "Why doesn't anyone care about this situation like I do?" "I am such a screw-up!" "I am so disappointed with myself!"

5. **I value you.** *I understand how you feel/how big this is for you.* Appreciation building: (Write about what God sees and enjoys about you. What do you sense God saying about how he sees you?)

   You sense that remembering things that bring joy or peace is good for you. Your heart opens to let Me and others in. You see a bit of the goodness and thankfulness that I built your heart to savor, remember, and share. You are feeling a little of my shalom—My warmth and joy as I look at you and am grateful for how you received this gift from Me. I have planned to bring you this moment all along. I enjoy watching you encounter and remember good things.

   Problem-resolution example: (God sees how overwhelming this situation is for you. He understands how you feel. What is God saying to you about it?)

   I understand how overwhelmed you feel by this situation. It feels daunting to you—as if you may sink under the weight of this problem. You feel the same way you did when your mom had her accident. I understand why you feel so unhappy about this. I can see you are shaken. I understand how troubled you are. Your feelings make sense to Me.

6. **I am glad to be with you and look upon your weakness with tenderness.** (Write about what you perceive God saying to you in His kind, tender, loving, and compassionate way.)
   Appreciation-building example:

   Your mind wants to get busy and distracted, so you don't think about this. Sometimes you feel like you must do something to make yourself more pleasing or valuable to me or others. Notice again how your thankful heart brings out some of the best things I created in you.

You are full of love, generosity, mercy, hope, and kindness. Sense My pride, and let Me smile at you just a while longer.

Problem-resolution example:

I am always glad to be with you. I am always delighted to interact with you, even when you find yourself in the midst of intense pain, frustration, or sadness. I look on your weakness with all the strength of My great compassion, ____________________ *(name).*

7. **I can do something about what you are going through.** (Write about what you perceive God saying about how he'll be with you and assist you now.)

   Appreciation-building example:

   When you stop to appreciate and be grateful for My gifts to you, you experience how we are alike. Each moment your heart is thankful and open, more of what we both like best about you comes to life. There is even more goodness inside you that I want to grow. I would like to take you on a tour of all My grace in your life so we can savor each memory together.

   Problem-resolution example:

   I can do something with and for you in this situation. I am here to strengthen you with My grace because you are special to Me. Remember how your friend made you feel so loved and cared for last week? Remember the specifics of how I have shown up to be with you in the past? In this present moment, I am with you in the same way, working for and in you. I will continue to provide you with this kind of encouragement.

   Take as much time as you would like for steps 8 and 9.

8. **MAKER PROMPT**. With the medium of your choice, capture the sum of your reflections. Let it be an expression of

what God's lovingkindness has created in you as a result of this time. (You may want to use one of the new skills you learned from reading this book.)

9. **SHARE** what you have made with your small group or someone you know and love. Sharing turns on mirror neurons that create connections and help form identity. Remember: this is not about creating a "perfect" project. It is about capturing an encounter you have had with Jesus and sharing the story. How did he meet you today? General guidelines:
   - When you share what you've created, provide only as much backstory as necessary to describe your experience. There is no need to explain or justify what the Lord impressed on your heart. Trust Holy Spirit.
   - When you tell someone you want to share your experience with the Integrating Immanuel Creativity exercise, let them know you do not want them to offer advice or ask questions. Concerning what you have shared, their job is merely to reflect God's heart for you on their face. And maybe give you a good hug.
   - Be sure to do step 9—sharing is too important to skip. Community amplifies and ripples out. Simply share what you've recorded for each of the other steps.

APPENDIX

FEELING WORDS AND EMOTIONS

The memories we feel and that stir our emotions make our stories "sticky"—stories that are stuck closely in our hearts and easily passed on to affix in the minds of others. Often in a story's retelling, we may forget to concisely convey these vital elements. Most adults aren't in the habit of using feeling words. Maybe it's because a lot of us struggle with emotions and the honest awareness of them.

We can up our connection with ourselves and others by identifying what we are feeling and where these feelings register in our body as we experience something memorable. As a result, our emotional vocabulary is pretty limited as is the depth of our story. (For instance, "Watching my daughter and her baby together made me smile" versus "I felt a warm, nurturing swell in my chest, my gaze lovingly softened, and a reflexive smile crossed my lips as I watched my daughter care for her baby. I felt like wrapping my arms around them both—protecting us all from ever losing the sweetness of this phase in our lives.") Learning to distinguish our emotional experiences and physical sensations helps us Assess our experience and build Awareness. Such honest, compassionate reflection enables us to better connect with others. Our right- and left-brain-dominant functions collaborate in the telling of rich stories—enabling us to know and be known.

What follows is a list of feeling words to undergird the structure of your story and strengthen the interaction with whomever is listening. Find one or two feeling words to capture and enrich each component of the stories you decide tell.

A

Abandoned, Able, Absorbed, Addled, Admired, Admirable, Affable, Affectionate, Afraid, Aggravated, Agreeable, Aggressive, Alive, Alarmed, Amazed, Ambivalent, Amused, Angry, Annoyed, Anxious, Appreciated, Appreciative, Apprehensive, Argumentative, Ashamed, Assured, Astonished, Attached, Aware, Awkward, Awed

B

Baffled, Bashed, Bashful, Beat, Beaten-up, Bereaved, Betrayed, Bewildered, Big, Bitter, Blessed, Blissful, Blue, Boggled, Bold, Brave, Bothered, Buoyant, Burdened

C

Calm, Cantankerous, Capable, Carefree, Caring, Careful, Cautious, Chagrined, Chaotic, Charitable, Cheerful, Cold, Compassionate, Complacent, Composed, Compulsive, Concerned, Confident, Connected, Considerate, Constricted, Contemptuous, Content, Contrite, Cooperative, Cranky, Crestfallen, Cross, Crushed, Curious

D

Daring, Defeated, Deceived, Defensive, Defiant, Dejected, Delighted, Demoralized, Depressed, Despairing, Desperate, Despondent, Detached, Determined, Devastated, Devious, Disappointed, Discouraged, Disdainful, Disenchanted, Disengaged, Disgraced, Disgusted, Disheartened, Disillusioned, Disinterested, Dismayed, Dismissed, Dismissive, Disorganized, Displayed, Distant, Distracted, Distraught, Distressed, Doleful, Doubtful, Dominated, Drained, Dreadful

E

Eager, Ease, Ecstatic, Edgy, Elated, Emboldened, Embarrassed, Empathetic, Empty, Encouraged, Energized, Enraged, Enthusiastic, Envious, Euphoric, Excited, Exasperated, Exhausted, Exploited, Extravagant, Exuberant.

F

Fair, Fatigued, Fearful, Flattered, Flustered, Foggy, Foolish, Forgiving, Fortunate, Frantic, Free, Frightened, Frozen, Frustrated, Fulfilled, Fuming, Funny, Furious, Fussy

G

Generous, Glad, Good, Gleeful, Gloomy, Glum, Gracious, Grateful, Gratified, Greedy, Grief, Grievous, Grumpy, Grief-stricken, Grouchy, Guarded, Guilty

H

Happy, Harassed, Hateful, Heartbroken, Helpless, Hesitant, Hopeful, Hopeless, Horrified, Hostile, Humbled, Humiliated, Hurt, Hyperactive, Hysterical,

I

Ignorant, Ignored, Immobilized, Impatient, Inadequate, Incensed, Indifferent, Impertinent, Inquisitive, Insecure, Insignificant, Inspired, Inspiring, Interested, Intimidated, Invisible, Irked, Irrational, Irritated, Irritable, Isolated

Jaded, Jealous, Jittery, Jocular, Joyful, Joyous, Jubilant, Judged, Judgmental, Justified

Kind, Keen

L

Lackluster, Lazy, Leery, Lethargic, Life-giving, Listless, Lonely, Loved, Loving

M

Mad, Malevolent, Manic, Manipulated, Manipulative, Marvelous, Mean, Meek, Melancholy, Melodramatic, Merciful, Mirthful, Mischievous, Miserable, Misunderstood, Moody, Mopey, Moved, Morose, Mournful

N

Naive, Nasty, Naughty, Needy, Needed, Neglected, Neglectful, Nervous, Nice, Nonchalant, Nonplussed, Numb

O

Obedient, Obligated, Obsessed, Obsessive, Obstinate, Offended, Open, Openminded, Optimistic, Outraged, Overjoyed, Overloaded, Overpowered, Overstimulated, Overwhelmed

P

Panicked, Passive, Panicky, Peaceful, Peeved, Pensive, Perplexed, Perturbed, Petrified, Petty, Petulant, Pissed, Pitiful, Placid, Playful, Pleased, Pleasure, Powerful, Powerless, Preoccupied, Pressured, Prickly, Prideful, Proud, Provoked, Puzzled

Q

Qualified, Quarrelsome, Quiet, Quirky, Quivery, Querulous

R

Rational, Rattled, Reasonable, Reasoned, Reassured, Rebellious, Refreshed, Regretful, Rejuvenated, Relaxed, Relieved, Reluctant, Remorseful, Repulsed, Resentful, Reserved, Resigned, Resolved, Respected, Restless, Ridiculed

S

Sabotaged, Sad, Safe, Sanguine, Sarcastic, Satisfied, Scared, Scornful, Secure, Seen, Seething, Sensitive, Serene, Serious, Shaken, Shalom, Shameful, Shy, Silly, Sincere, Skeptical, Smothered, Smug, Sociable, Sorrowful, Spiteful, Stagnant, Startled, Stifled, Stressed, Stubborn, Stuck, Stunned, Sympathetic, Surprised, Suspicious, Swamped

T

Tearful, Teary, Temperamental, Tender, Tense, Terrible, Terrific, Terrified, Thankful, Thoughtful, Threatened, Thoughtful, Thrilled, Throttled, Tickled, Timid, Tired, Tiresome, Tolerant, Tolerated, Tormented, Torn, Touched, Trapped, Tranquil, Troubled, Trusted, Trusting, Trustworthy

U

Unafraid, Unappreciated, Uncertain, Uncomfortable, Undecided, Uneasy, Unhappy, Unimpressed, Unloved, Unnerved, Unrestricted, Unruffled, Unruly, Unseen, Unsteady, Unsettled, Unsure, Unwanted, Uplifted, Upset, Uptight, Used, Useful, Useless

V

Vacant, Vain, Valued, Valuable, Vengeful, Vexed, Vibrant, Victimized, Victorious, Vindictive, Violent, Vital, Vivacious, Volatile, Vulnerable

W

Warm, Wary, Wasted, Weak, Weary, Weepy, Whimsical, Whiny, Willful, Willing, Wistful, Wishful, Witty, Withdrawn, Woeful, Worldly, Worn, Worried, Worthless, Wronged, Wounded

Y

Young, Youthful, Yielding, Yearning

Z

Zany, Zealous, Zestful

MAKER AFFIRMATIONS

Maker's Affirmation 1 ***(based on Psalm 27:13–14):***

Makers care profoundly about the redemptive needs of the world that cause their soul to grieve—they make as a compassionate expression of their care for others. **I am a maker.**

Maker's Affirmation 2 ***(based on Genesis 1:26–28):***

Makers value their own experiences, feelings, and emotions as essential fodder for their creative life with God. This awareness cracks open their souls to make room for His redemptive work. **I am a maker.**

Maker's Affirmation 3 ***(based on 1 Corinthians 8:3):***

Makers share themselves deeply—connecting with God and others out of a desire to know them, be known, and to participate in the ongoing process of spiritual transformation. **I am a maker.**

Maker's Affirmation 4 ***(based on Colossians 3:15–17):***

Makers establish shalom—a balanced sense of peace and joyful anticipation with God—before taking creative action with left-brain formulas or processes. **I am a maker.**

Maker's Affirmation 5 ***(based on Exodus 3:2–4):***

Makers slow down in order to open themselves up to what God wants to focus attention on. **I am a maker.**

Maker Affirmation 6 (based on Philippians 4:6–7):

Makers reject a life of dark despair. Instead, they relax in the light of God's love, care, and community.

Maker's Affirmation 7 *(based on Isaiah 41:10):*

Makers process fearful emotions with God and others on the spiritual journey. Recognizing and sharing creative struggles reminds them that they are never alone. **I am a maker.**

Maker's Affirmation 8 *(based on 2 Corinthians 12:9–10):*

Makers keep grace-based bearings—spontaneously expressing their undeserved blessings and sharing treasures gifted to them by God. **I am a maker.**

Maker's Affirmation 9 *(based on 1 Peter 3:15):*

Makers testify with the stories they tell and the transformational life they live.

Maker's Affirmation 10 *(based on Isaiah 55:12):*

Makers cultivate inspiration by enjoying a fun, full, magnetic life balance. **I am a maker.**

Maker's Affirmation 11 *(based on Matthew 5:16):*

Makers holistically glorify God, drawing others to Him through their authentic way of being. **I am a maker.**

Maker's Affirmation 12 *(based on Psalm 149:1):*

Makers hold their redemptive purpose humbly before God, themselves, and others—inviting collaboration for a kingdom cause. **I am a maker.**

WHAT ATTACHMENT STYLE ARE YOU?

God designed our souls for connection and delight in being with others. Who we love shapes our identity more than anything else. With our basic needs for comfort and security met, we develop a sense of value and independence—a healthy identity empowered to successfully navigate relationships with boldness, curiosity, and joy. Generally, we are better at seeking, receiving, and giving support.

The level of responsiveness and availability of the primary caregiver in our first three years of life creates the attachment style we see in our relationships today—even in our relationship with God. Secure attachment is a balance of grace-based, loving trust that grows our emotional and psychological capacity to form healthy self-esteem. Our caregiver demonstrated their delight in being with us and gave us important proof that we were special to them—fuel for a joyful identity.

Whatever our experience, you and I must know where we stand in this regard. We tend to carry this attachment style into adulthood.

So what if, like many, our primary caregiver wasn't responsive or connected with us during those critical years? How do we know what kind of insecure attachment we may have, and what can we do about it?

The first step is recognizing our type. The three insecure attachment types include Avoidant, Anxious, and Disorganized. Each of these is rooted in fear and counterproductive to a thriving life with God and others.

Without taking too deep of a dive, I'll define each insecure style in terms of life balance:

- **Avoidant insecure attachment** types experience neglect in their early years. They tend to play alone as children and, as they grow, commonly describe themselves as "independent." Generally loners, Avoidants don't put much stock in relationships either. Staying siloed in their heads allows them to avoid life stress and conflict by distancing themselves—turning inward, withdrawing, and remaining emotionally aloof. It is easier than the disappointment of continuing unmet needs.
- **Anxious insecure attachment**. A caregiver's unpredictable responsibility and availability create distrust in a young child—it's understandably confusing. As a result, they commonly develop self-doubt and a preoccupation with seeking approval and reassurance from other people. Rejection seems crouched behind every door, driving them to clinginess and distrust in their meaningful relationships.
- **Disorganized insecure attachment.** Growing up in traumatic or chaotic homes creates a fearful attachment base. Distancing themselves from their feelings—especially during traumatic episodes—taught them to distrust and detach from themselves. Fear of the caregiver offsets their desire for love and care. When the emotions of past wounds are triggered, they resurface as if they are in the present. Someone with disorganized attachment has a disordered sense of self and confusing connections with others.

The good news? What is wounded in community can be healed in community—*only* in community. While it isn't easy, insecure attachments can be rewired with secure, healthy attachments—and it is worth the relational risk. I recommend adopting a gratitude practice, the discipline of Scripture-centered breath prayer, and the guidance of an Emotionally Focused Therapist. In the meantime, become aware of where insecurity takes residence in your body, mind, and emotions by paying attention to patterns of feelings and reactions. Focusing on developing healthy relational habits and maturity can lead to the freedom and spiritual growth for which we are made. Our character, identity, connection, and life with God depend on it.

YOUR HEART SONG AND CREATIVE GREAT COMMISSION

The following is designed to help you prayerfully discern the tune of your heart song and the enduring purpose of your creative Great Commission.

Your Enduring Lament:

"The seed of any creative action is lament." – Andy Crouch

An enduring longing or yearning embodied within your journey.

Have you ever considered how lament has inspired you to creative action?

Your Maker's Heart Song:

What are the lyrics of persistent message in your heart, soul, and mind? What undeniable truth has God taught you that makes "your heart burn within" (Luke 24:13–35)? (Hint: you have probably often found yourself in a position to share your song already.)

Your lament + your joy-based heart song + your skillset/talents/gifting = your heart song

(Note: the context will evolve over the course of your life, but the message of your heart song will remain.)

Ask God to show you.

Your Purpose/Calling within the Great Commission:

Invitation (need) + discernment + community → make disciples

Scriptural Foundation:

"Let the peace of Christ keep you in tune with each other, in step with each other. None of this going off and doing your own thing. And cultivate thankfulness. Let the Word of Christ—the Message—have the run of the house. Give it plenty of room in your lives. Instruct and direct one another using good common sense. And sing, sing your hearts out to God! Let every detail in your lives—words, actions, whatever—be done in the name of the Master, Jesus, thanking God the Father every step of the way."

COLOSSIANS 3:16 (MSG)

Meanwhile, the eleven disciples were on their way to Galilee, headed for the mountain Jesus had set for their reunion. The moment they saw him they worshiped him. Some, though, held back, not sure about worship, about risking themselves totally.

Jesus, undeterred, went right ahead and gave his charge: "God authorized and commanded me to commission you: Go out and train everyone you meet, far and near, in this way of life, marking them by baptism in the threefold name: Father, Son, and Holy Spirit. Then instruct them in the practice of all I have commanded you. I'll be with you as you do this, day after day after day, right up to the end of the age."

MATTHEW 28:16–20 (MSG)

REFLECTION

1. Enduring Lament – How has an enduring lament inspired creative action in you?

   Is there a song of lament in Scripture that you resonate with within that area?

2. Gratitude – In any way, are you grateful for what that lament has offered you?

   Consider the gifts God and others have given you. Make a list and as you do, picture each in your mind's eye. Revisit the person, place, or thing with all your senses. How do you feel about each in your physical body and emotions?

3. Heart Song – Is there a redemptive theme or message that God has made central in your life—a "song" you frequently find yourself "singing" to encourage others in their life with God?

4. What purpose do you hear the Lord calling you into in this season? Is it consistent with the message of your heart song? Where have you sensed doors opening or closing?

   If you find this hard tot put your finger on right now, ask God to show you where He is inviting you to sing your heart song. Ask Him to show you a reflection of this purpose in His Word. Now, pay attention and seek discernment.

5. Create something that captures your heart song and creative Great Commission.

FEATURED MAKERS

Many thanks to the artists whose generous friendship and collaboration brought joy to my heart and these pages. Find out more of what motivates their making and how to contact them below.

To enrich your creative experience of their work, you can see full-color versions of each piece by visiting AmyPierson.com. Use code **MAKEMORE** to unlock this content and more!

Carol Aust, (2021), *Breaking Bread,* acrylics on canvas.
Website: carolaust.com Instagram: @carolaust
Email: art@carolaust.com

My figurative paintings are emotionally charged narrative fragments infused with mysterious tension and secrecy. I want to leave room for the viewer to insert their own story. Often, I place the figures in precarious environments where anything could happen. Sometimes celebratory, sometimes lonely and disturbing, my paintings express a wide range of human desire and yearning. I consistently combine strong and vibrant colors along with my figures—making them both engaging and vulnerable. Perhaps this is how God sees and knows us—teaching us to see and know one another?

Jenny Freeman, (2021), *Foggy Day,* oil on canvas.
Instagram: @jennifersfreeman

The process of painting teaches me to slow down, to "look and see" on many levels. As an artist, I am a student of light—constantly looking for and trying to capture how it falls on my subject. Without light there are no values or color. I can't help but think of the biblical metaphors. The psalmist says, "In Your light we see light." In the gospel of John, Jesus says, "I am the light of the world. Whoever follows me will never walk in darkness, but will have the light of life" (John 8:12 NIV). *God is light.* We are totally dependent on light not only to paint or draw but to live. I am hopelessly dependent on God's light to paint the canvas of my life. His light "illuminates my darkness," the psalmist declares. His light gives me the ability to discern correct values, have confident "brushstrokes" or choices with intentional boundaries, focus, and purpose. Only with Him is my world is colored with gratitude and joy.

Gayla Irwin, *Stalking Bear* (2022), watercolor.
website: GaylaIrwin.com Instagram: @gaylairwinart

I am on a mission to cultivate joy, beauty, and wholeness through contemplative creativity. Creating with watercolors, ink, in my art journal, or on my iPad brings me great delight. I want to help others experience this delight, too.

Debra Komodore, *Walking on Water* (2023), mixed media.
Email: d.komodore@comcast.net

Living life's journey as a visual artist joyfully engages me through an inner world of imagination, discovery, and creation.

These wonder-full yet vulnerable moments humble me in the presence of God's gentle and loving spirit Spirit—there, I find a place of insight and life-giving energy where time stands still. For me, making is "a magical confluence of playfulness, connection, and flow."

Christa MacFarlane, *Seeing Beyond* (2020), acrylics on canvas.
Website: ChristaMacfarlane.com Instagram: Christa MacFarlane Art
Facebook: Christa MacFarlane Art Email: christa@christamacfarlane.com

Sacred places can look very different to many different people. Everyone needs a place that provides serenity and hope, a place to see beyond our current circumstances. Connecting with God's creation in nature brings it all into focus for me, trusting that there is something larger and more powerful than myself. Reflecting on my own interpretations while painting the tiniest of weeds reminds me that we all have a purpose on this earth. This gives me a deeper connection with God, my Creator, and strengthens my faith. It certainly is humbling and brings me peace.

Julie McKnight, *Soaring Soul* (2021) and *Aslan's Tale* (2017), composite digital art.
Website: AlpenglowStudios.com Instagram: @jmmdesign
Email: jmm@silverstar.com

This John O'Donohue quote inspires my art: "Simply by being still and silent, by coming into the stillness of your own heart, you will find the God that is waiting there within you for your arrival home."

I carry the wonder of a child who is dazzled by God. As such, I am constantly looking for ways to interact and partner with God to express His heart for His kids. Using the language of the arts, I hope for others to sense and respond to His invitation to see Him with the eyes of their heart.

Sue Shehan, *Bountiful* (2013), soft pastels on paper.
Email: sueshehan@me.com

As I look at landscapes, clouds, skies, and forests, I am reminded that my Creator is with me. As He manifests His glory through nature, I am moved and inspired to express myself in ways that reflect Him.

Elaine St. Louis, *Golden Bowl* (2017), acrylic on panel.
Website: ElaineStLouis.com Instagram: @ejstlouis
Email: ejstlouis@msn.com Etsy: ElaineStLouisArt

Throughout my life, even since I was very small, I've always felt "guided" whenever I create. Sometimes, I become so fascinated in watching the subject come alive on the canvas or board that I actually drop my brush. Kind of a little "God mic-drop"! In making my observations of creation into a tangible piece, I feel such a connection with the Creator. In a way, my work is giving thanks for His gift by reflecting it back to Him in my own voice.

John Woods, *Rubber Band Ball* (2021), oil on canvas.
Website: JohnWoodsStudio.com Instagram:@johnwoodsstudio

I believe art is about flourishing—no art, no joy. It enlivens and enlarges your vision of who you are and what you can achieve. With that said, our lives are our biggest project, yet most of us exercise but a fraction of our capacity to express ourselves in the world.

NOTES

1 Trevor Hudson, *Hope Beyond Your Tears: Experiencing Christ's Healing Love* (United States: Upper Room Books, 2012), 15.

2 Brené Brown, "Wholehearted Living" (PhD diss., University of Houston, 2006).

3 Moshe Bar, *Mindwandering: How Constant Mental Drift Can Improve Your Mood and Boost Your Creativity,* (New York: Hachette Book Group, 2022), 9.

4 Marcus Warner and Jim Wilder, *Rare Leadership: Four Uncommon Habits for Increasing Trust, Joy, and Engagement in the People You Lead* (Chicago: Moody Press, 2016), 66-68.

5 Dallas Willard, *Renovation of the Heart* (Colorado Springs: NavPress, 2002), 161.

6 Peter & Geri Scazzero, Emotionally Healthy Spirituality: It's Impossible to Be Spiritually Mature, While Remaining Emotionally Immature (Grand Rapids, MI: Zondervan, 2014), 9.

7 Scazzero, Emotionally Healthy Spirituality, 44-45.

8 Amishi P. Jha, PhD, "How to Tame Your Wandering Mind," filmed March 2017 at TEDxCoconutGrove, Coconut Grove, FL, video, 18:08, https://youtu.be/UQzvNIIMayo .

9 "Nurtured by Nature," American Psychological Association, Monitor on Psychology, 51(3), last modified April 1, 2020, https://www.apa.org/monitor/2020/04/nurtured-nature/.

10 Alan Schore, "Early organization of the nonlinear right brain and development of a predisposition to psychiatric disorders," Development and Psychopathology, 9(4) (1997), https://doi.org/10.1017/s0954579497001363/.

11 Jon Acuff. "Build Your Awesome Life" Course. Week 3. May 13, 2022.

12 Stephen Pressfield, *The War of Art: Break Through the Blocks and Win Your Inner Creative Battles* (New York: Black Irish Entertainment, 2002), 14.

13 Ed Khouri, *Becoming a Face of Grace: Navigating Lasting Relationship with God and Others* (United States: Illumify Global Media, 2021), 171-172.

14 Bessel a. Van der Kolk, *The Body Keeps the Score: Brain, Mind, and Body in the Healing of Trauma* (New York: Penguin Books, 2014), 45.

15 E. James Wilder, Anna Kang, John Loppnow, Sungshim Loppnow, *Joyful Journey: Listening to Immanuel* (East Peoria, IL: Shepherd's House, 2015), 47-51.

16 Andrew Murray, *Humility* (New Kensington, PA: Whitaker House, 1982), 15-16.

17 Hans urs von Balthasar, *The Glory of the Lord: A Theological Aesthetics, Vol. 1, Seeing the Form* (United Kingdom: T. & T. Clark, 1982).

18 Timothy D. Willard, *The Beauty Chasers: Recapturing the Wonder of the Divine* (Grand Rapids, MI: Zondervan Reflective, 2022), 10-11.

19 Brené Brown, *The Gifts of Imperfection* (Center City, MN: Hazelden Publishing, 2020) 102-103, 165-166.

20 Brené Brown, *Daring Greatly: How the Courage to Be Vulnerable Transforms the Way We Live, Love, Parent, and Lead* (New York: Avery Publishing, 2012*)*, 37.

21 Madeline L'Engle, *Walking on Water: Reflections on Faith & Art* (New York: Penguin Random House, 2016), 37.

22 Khouri, *Face of Grace*, 171.

23 Stuart Brown, MD, *Play: How It Shapes the Brian, Opens the Imagination, and Invigorates the Soul* (London: Penguin Publishing Group, 2009), 16-18, Kindle.

24 Brown, *Play*, 104.

25 David P. Fessell and Karen Reivich, "Why You Need to Protect Your Sense of Wonder — Especially Now," *Harvard Business Review*, August 25, 2021, https://hbr.org/2021/08/why-you-need-to-protect-your-sense-of-wonder-especially-now/.

26 Brennan Manning, *The Furious Longing of God.* (Colorado Springs: David C Cook, 2009), 97.

27 Curt Thompson, MD, *The Soul of Desire: Discovering the Neuroscience of Longing, Beauty, and Community* (Downers Grove, IL: InterVarsity Press, 2021), 49.

ABOUT THE AUTHOR

Amy Pierson is a writer and champion of creativity for lasting spiritual transformation. She formerly served as executive director of the Spiritual Formation Alliance and founded Burning Heart Workshops (a soul care ministry combining classic spiritual formation, neurotheology, and creative soul care). Amy is a graduate of the Renovaré Institute for Christian Spiritual Formation/ Santa Barbara Cohort, an advisory partner with Dallas Willard Ministries, a curriculum contributor for Unhurried Living's Replenish Coaching Community, a ministry intercessor, and is active in Denver's Downing House community.

She received her Bachelor of Science in journalism and advertising from the University of Colorado, Boulder. A writer, speaker, artist, mom, and "Ama" (still hard to believe), Amy lives in the Denver area with her hilarious husband, Bill, and their ridiculous golden retriever.

Printed in the USA
CPSIA information can be obtained
at www.ICGtesting.com
LVHW031132230224
772606LV00046B/874